PRACTICAL AND PRECISE TRIVIA

by

BECKY COLEBANK

TABLE OF CONTENTS

ANCIENT HISTORY

1. What Roman author and philosopher died while watching the eruption of Mount Vesuvius in 79 A.D?   **A: Pliny the Elder**

2. What famed 5th century philosopher's works are known chiefly through the writings of his students, Plato and Aristotle?

A: Socrates

3. Which of the Seven Wonders of the Ancient World was a 100-foot tall statue of the Greek sun god Helios?   **A: Colossus of Rhodes**

4. The name of this ancient citadel or fortified building literally meant "upper city" in Greek.   **A: Acropolis**

5. What ancient road connecting Rome with Brindisi, Apulia was named after Appius Claudius Caecus, the Roman censor who built the first section?   **A: Appian Way**

6. What subterranean chambers were used as burial vaults for early Christians?   **A: Catacombs**

7. What is the name of the Roman wall that runs across northern England?   **A: Hadrian's Wall**

8. What boy king's mummy went on display in his underground tomb in the Valley of the Kings in Luxor in 2007, 85 years after discovery by Howard Carter and George Herbert, 5th Earl of Carnarvon?   **A: King Tutankhamen**

9. What was the Latin term for the 206-year span of "Roman Peace" established in the 1st century A.D. by Emperor Augustus?

A: Pax Romana or Pax Augustus

10. What ancient South American culture flourished in the Andes from 1438 to 1533?   **A: The Incas**

11. What Roman ruler's mother Aurelia successfully lived through childbirth, proving false the legend that he was the first person born by Caesarean section?   **A: Julius Caesar**

12. What Egyptian king's trumpet was tooted on the radio in 1939, 3,297 years after his death?   **A: King Tut**

13. The Great Pyramid of Giza, one of the Seven Wonders of the Ancient World, was commissioned as a tomb for this Egyptian pharaoh.   **A: Cheops (or Khufu)**

14. What legendary Thracian slave led a revolt against Rome in 73 BC?   **A: Spartacus**

15. What is the term for a conical pile of stones raised as a memorial over a burial in prehistoric times?   **A: Cairn**

16. What ancient Roman emperor with a reputation for cruel autocracy wore military boots as a child, earning him the nickname "little boot"?   **A: Caligula**

17. What was the term for a body of three to six thousand soldiers in ancient Rome?   **A: Legion**

18. What ancient King of Mesopotamia was known for putting the laws of his country into a formal written code?
A: Hammurabi

19. What is the term for the 15th day of March, May, July or October or the 13th day of the other months in the ancient Roman calendar?   **A: Ides**

20. This term for a character of the ancient Egyptian writing system comes from the Greek for "sacred writing."   **A: Hieroglyph**

21. What is the proper term for a native or inhabitant of ancient Troy?   **A: Trojan**

22. What stratovolcano in the Gulf of Naples covered Pompeii with lava in AD 79?   **A: Vesuvius**

23. Ancient Hebrew law established every 50th year as a year of emancipation of slaves and restoration of lands to former owners. What was this year called?   **A: Jubilee**

24. This area of the Tigris–Euphrates river system is widely considered to be the cradle of civilization in the West.

A: Mesopotamia

25. This king of Macedon, considered to be one of history's most successful military commanders, was tutored until the age of 16 by the philosopher Aristotle.   **A: Alexander the Great or Alexander III of Macedon**

ANIMALS

1. Members of this African antelope genus, which includes wildebeests, have curved horns, ox-like heads, and long tails.

A: Gnu

2. What is the proper term for a baby oyster?   **A: Spat**

3. The name of this snake, the world's longest, is "Ophiophagus" which means "snake-eater."   **A: King cobra**

4. The legs of this Minnesota state bird are so far back on the body they are clumsy on land and go there only to nest.

A: Loons or divers

5. The Northern variety of these long, jawless fish related to eels and hagfish have the highest number of chromosomes among vertebrates.   **A: Lampreys**

6. What arctic rodents are mistakenly thought to commit mass suicide when they migrate?   **A: Lemmings**

7. These elongated creatures can be sawtooth, spaghetti or moray.   **A: Eels**

8. This carnivorous animal with the binomial name "ursus maritimus" can detect seals buried under three feet of snow nearly a mile away.   **A: Polar bear**

9. What taxonomical suborder consists of mammals which chew their cud?   **A: Ruminants**

10. This largest member of the dolphin family often lives in

Stable matrilineal family groups that pass hunting techniques and vocal behaviors from generation to generation.   **A: Killer whale or orca**

11. The common name for these massive bovines came from French fur trappers who called them "boeufs," meaning ox or bullock.   **A: Buffalo or bison**

12. The largest recorded nest ever built by this bird of prey was located in Florida in 1963. It was 10 feet wide and 20 feet deep. **A: Bald eagle**

13. Many hummingbird species go into this nightly state of reduced metabolism.   **A: Torpor**

14. A "squab" is a baby _____.   **A: Pigeon**

15. This breed of gun dog gets its name from its distinctive crouch upon finding its quarry.   **A: Setter**

16. Carnivores that primarily eat insects and similar invertebrates are called _____.   **A: Insectivores**

17. What large feline is the world's fastest land animal, running 70 to 75 miles per hour in short bursts?   **A: Cheetah**

18. What bird comprises up to 80% of a peregrine falcon's diet in urban areas?   **A: (Rock) pigeons**

19. What dog breed has higher levels of red blood cells than other breeds, allowing it to excel at "coursing" deer and hare? **A: Greyhound**

20. Due to its long, stout claws and extreme musculature, an adult one of these omnivorous mammals can dig a hole faster than a man with a shovel.   **A: Badger**

21. What breed of cat can have blue, chocolate, lilac or seal "points"?   **A: Siamese**

22. These venomous fiddleback spiders are hard to eradicate because of their ability to live several seasons with no food or water and to survive after losing limbs.   **A: Brown recluse**

23. This reptile's name come from the Greek phrase meaning "lizard of the Nile."   **A: Crocodile**

24. These lizards have specialized cells called chromatophores, which contain pigments that allow them to change their skin coloration.   **A: Chameleon**

25. Cetaceans (whales, porpoises, dolphins) swim in social groups called what?   **A: Pods**

26. What North American ruminants have the largest antlers relative to body size among living deer species?   **A: Caribou**

27. Songwriters have adopted this bird as a symbol of happiness and cheer, as in "Somewhere Over the Rainbow."
A: Bluebird

28. What large working dog breed was originally bred for rescue in the Italian and Swiss Alps?   **A: St. Bernard**

29. What is the common name for the "Ursus Horribilus" of western North America?   **A: Grizzly bear**

30. What breed of wiry-coated dog has a name which literally

means "snout" in German?   **A: Schnauzer**

31. What is the proper term for a baby elephant?   **A: Calf**

32. In what mountain range might you find a vicuña in its natural habitat?   **A: Andes**

33. What sitcom which ran from 1993 to 2004 featured a Jack Russell terrier which made the breed surge in American Kennel Club registrations?   **A: Frasier**

34. Pandas spend about 12 hours per day eating 20 to 40 pounds of this fibrous plant.   **A: Bamboo**

35. Chickens which are not kept in cages and which are allowed to roam free are called this.   **A: Free range**

36. What "F" word describes the back part of a horse's leg just above the hoof?   **A: Fetlock**

37. This mammal is not only the largest existing animal – it is the heaviest that ever existed.   **A: Blue whale**

38. What reptiles have a reflex that causes their eyes to tear up when they open their mouths, thus making it look as though they are crying while eating their prey?   **A: Crocodiles**

39. What genetic hybrid was created because thousands of cattle died in a Kansas blizzard in 1886?   **A: Beefalo or cattalo**

40. What type of camel has only one hump?   **A: Dromedary**

41. In 1929, this animal movie star received the most votes for the Best Actor Oscar, but the Academy felt a human should win.

A: Rin Tin Tin

42. What Algonquian word for turtle is used to describe several types of small, hard-shell turtles typically found in brackish waters?   **A: Terrapin**

43. The largest living chelonian is this type of sea turtle which can reach a weight of over 2,000 lbs.   **A: Leatherback**

44. This bird activity is vital for keeping plumage oily, water-repellent and insulating.   **A: Preening**

45. By the time his egg hatches, the male of this penguin species will have fasted for around 115 days.   **A: Emperor penguin**

46. What is the term for a sexually mature female hog prior to having her first litter?   **A: Gilt**

47. There are around 85,000 species of these marine organisms which are divided into cephalopods and gastropods.

A: Mollusks

48. The digestive processes of this South American arboreal mammal take nearly a month to complete.   **A: Sloth**

49. Oology is the branch of ornithology that deals with the study of _____.   **A: Eggs**

50. What disaster killed an estimated 580,000 birds in Prince William Sound, Alaska in 1989?   **A: Exxon Valdez oil spill**

51. What is the term for cattle which have been dehorned, either naturally or otherwise?   **A: Polled**

52. All male whales of this species within the North Atlantic area sing the same song, while those in the North Pacific all sing another song.   **A: Humpback**

53. Baleen whales often feed on these small crustaceans whose name comes from the Norwegian meaning "young fry of fish."

A: Krill

54. What is the proper term for a female horse less than four or five years old?   **A: Filly**

55. What variety of tuna can grow to 6 and a half feet in length and live for 50 years?   **A: Bluefin**

56. What is the proper term for a male pig castrated before reaching sexual maturity?   **A: Barrow**

57. What term describes a species that was once domesticated and has since reverted to a free-roaming life in the wild?   **A: Feral**

58. What is the state bird of New Mexico (also known as the ground cuckoo?   **A: Roadrunner**

59. What is the proper term for a castrated male sheep?

A: Wether

60. What is the proper term for a young pigeon?   **A: Squab**

61. What crustaceans have blue blood due to the presence of haemocyanin which contains copper?   **A: Lobster**

62. What large fish are the most valuable of all harvested fish due to the demand for their roe?   **A: Sturgeons**

63. These mammals, the last surviving members of the order Cingulata, are often used in leprosy research.   **A: Armadillos**

64. What is the proper term for a flock of quail?   **A: Bevy**

65. What was the name of Richard Nixon's cocker spaniel that he mentioned in his famous 1952 speech defending his political contributions?   **A: Checkers**

66. These large mammals, whose closest relatives are dugongs and manatees, are the sole remaining family within the order "Proboscidea."   **A: Elephants**

67. What seabird has a wing span of up to 14 feet and only needs to land once every couple of years to breed?   **A: Albatross**

68. What African mammal was prized by Zulu warriors for its bravery, unmatched even by lions in its courage?

A: Hippopotamus

69. What mammal is nearly invisible to an infrared camera due to its superb insulation and transparent fur?   **A. Polar bear**

70. This large breed of dog is a descendant of working and hunting dogs kept by the Kobuk group of Inupiat of upper western Alaska.

A: Malamute

71. These Central and South American reptiles resemble a small alligator.   **A: Caiman or cayman**

72. A "mahout" is the driver of a/an _____.   **A: Elephant**

73. What hornless sheep with short, thick wool is named after a hilly area in England?   **A: Cheviot**

74. What toothless, spiny, egg-laying, burrowing animal is only found in Australia?   **A: Echidna**

75. What domesticated ox of Asia and Africa has a prominent hump and a large dewlap?   **A: Zebu**

ARCHITECTURE AND BUILDING

1. There are three types of classical architectural columns: Ionic, Doric and this one.   **A: Corinthian**

2. What great American architect developed the prairie style of architecture in Chicago?   **A: Frank Lloyd Wright**

3. What is the general term for the architectural style characterized by pointed arches, ribbed vaulting, flying buttresses and grotesque decorations that was prevalent between the 12th and 16th centuries?   **A: Gothic**

4. What is the term for a roofed window set vertically on a sloping roof?   **A: Dormer**

5. What type of siding is made of thin horizontal wood planks, each one overlapping the next?   **A: Clapboard**

6. What medieval architectural style features decorative half-timbering and heavy chimneys?   **A: Tudor**

7. Some of the more famous examples of this spherical architectural structure are the Montreal Biosphere in Quebec, the aviary at the Queens Zoo in Flushing Meadows, and Spaceship Earth at the EPCOT Center in Walt Disney World.   **A: Geodesic Dome**

8. What is the term for a large, many-windowed building built to house potted orange trees during the winter?   **A: Orangery**

9. What American architect designed "Fallingwater" to be in

harmony with its environment?   **A: Frank Lloyd Wright**

10. These roof spouts are in the form of a grotesque or fantastic creature.   **A: Gargoyle**

11. This building term, used to describe insulation, is the measure of a material's capacity to impede heat flow.   **A: R-value**

12. Who was the architect of St. Paul's Cathedral in London?

A: Sir Christopher Wren

13. What is the term for the part of a steeple where bells are hung?   **A: Belfry**

14. From the French words for "gliding door," it's the term for an iron grating over a gateway.   **A: Portcullis**

15. This type of steel beam used in skyscrapers is so named because its cross section has the form of a certain capital letter.

A: I-beam

16. These large adobe structures in the Southwest were originally called the Castilian word for "town" or "village."   **A: Pueblo**

17. What American architect wrote, "No house should ever be on any hill or on anything. It should be OF the hill, belonging to it, so hill and house could live together each the happier for the other"?

A: Frank Lloyd Wright

18. No building may be built taller than this building in the city of Washington, D. C.   **A: The Capitol**

19. Danish architect Jørn Utzon won an international design competition to design this expressionist-style performing arts

center in Australia.   **A: Sydney Opera House**

20. At $100,000, this is the most lucrative award an architect can receive.   **A: Pritzker Architecture Prize**

ART

1. What French artist painted many depictions of Tahitian life, including "Tahitian Women on the Beach"? **A: Gaugin**

2. This early 20th century art movement rejected traditional art forms and concepts of beauty and expressed its cynicism through chaos and nonsense. **A: Dadaism**

3. What new abstract artistic movement was headed by Picasso and Braque between 1907 and 1914? **A: Cubism**

4. What 20th century American pop artist liked to pain Campbell's soup cans? **A: Andy Warhol**

5. This artist of the Dutch Golden Age created works that showed everyday life in the city of Delft in the Netherlands in the 17th century. **A: Vermeer**

6. In which Vatican City building will you find Michelangelo's "The Creation of Man"? **A: Sistine Chapel**

7. What major Spanish artist was born in Greece, hence his name? **A: El Greco**

8. What American pop artist created the big tongue which first appeared on the cover of the Rolling Stones' "Sticky Fingers" album? **A: Andy Warhol**

9. This statue sculpted by the French sculptor Rodin is known in France as "Le Penseur." **A: The Thinker**

10. What painting depicts the sister and the dentist of artist Grant Wood as rural farm folk? **A: American Gothic**

11. What is the term for a picture in which the subject's distinctive features or peculiarities are exaggerated for comic effect?

A: Caricature

12. What artist was 80 years old when her first solo public show launched her career as a major artist?   **A: Grandma Moses**

13. The selected group of colors an artist has chosen to use in a particular work of art is called his/her _____.

A: Palette

14. What type of painting shows objects such as flowers, food, or musical instruments, and reveals an artist's skill in painting shapes, light, and shadow?   **A: Still life**

15. A painting done on wet plaster on a wall is known as a

_____.   **A: Fresco**

16. In painting, this term means to apply small dots of color with the point of the brush.   **A: Stipple**

17. What highly decorative artistic style, popular at the end of the 19th and beginning of the 20th century, made heavy use of ornamentally curving lines and shapes derived from flower and plant motifs?   **A: Art Noveau**

18. This work is the most parodied and most famous of all Leonardo da Vinci's works.   **A: Mona Lisa**

19. What Renaissance painter was a vegetarian with a habit of buying caged birds and releasing them?   **A: Leonardo da Vinci**

20. What Early Renaissance painter was the creator of "The Birth of Venus" and "Primavera"?   **A: Sandro Botticelli**

21. What is the term for a repeating theme, image, or pattern in a work of art?   **A: Motif**

22. What is the term for the artistic technique of applying opaque watercolor to paper?   **A: Gouache**

23. Which Italian city was the center for Renaissance sculpting masters such as Michelangelo, Cellini, Donatello and the Della Robbia family?   **A: Florence**

24. What is the term for an artistic construction consisting of balanced parts capable of motion?   **A: Mobile**

25. What is the term for the artistic technique of covering a surface with cutouts such as paper?   **A: Decoupage**

26. What is the art term for a stick of pure powdered pigment held together with a binder?   **A: Pastel**

27. This artistic movement which stresses the weird, the irrational and the dreamworld grew out of the Dada movement in the 1920s.

A: Surrealism

28. Whose design for the Vietnam War Memorial was chosen to be built in Washington D.C. in 1982?   **A: Maya Lin**

29. Who painted "The Blue Boy"?   **A: Thomas Gainsborough**

30. What Dutch painter born in 1606 is considered one of the greatest painters in history for his unique use of light and shadow?

A: Rembrandt

31. What red-yellow color is named after the 16th-century Venetian painter who used it?   **A: Titian**

32. This post-Impressionist Frenchman's painting "The Card Players" sold for more than $250 million in 2011.   **A: Paul Cézanne**

33. Which artist has sold more works for more than a million dollars than any other?   **A: Picasso**

34. What famed 1937 painting by Picasso was a depiction of the bombing of a Basque town by German war planes in the Spanish Civil War?   **A: Guernica**

35. What English landscape painter painted "The Hay Wain" in 1821?   **A: John Constable**

36. Whose 1907 painting, "Les Demoiselles d'Avignon," was regarded as the first Cubist painting?   **A: Pablo Picasso**

37. What is the term for the artistic technique of applying a decoration cut from one material to the surface of another?   **A: Applique**

38. What artist's famed "Water Lilies" was the epitome of Impressionist painting?   **A: Claude Monet**

39. What 17th-century artist painted the picture that is now embossed on the lid of Dutch Masters Cigars?   **A: Rembrandt**

40. Almost all this 17th-century artist's paintings are set in two smallish rooms in his house in Delft.   **A: Johannes Vermeer**

ASTRONOMY

1. What type of star is the strongest magnet in the universe with a magnetic field a million million times stronger than Earth's magnetism?   **A: Neutron**

2. This radiation belt around the earth was named after an American physicist.   **A: Van Allen Belts**

3. What space location has a gravitational field too strong for light to escape?   **A: Black hole**

4. What name has become a stand-in term for scientists for any undiscovered planet in the outer Solar System?   **A: Planet X**

5. What is the term for a second full moon in a calendar month?   **A: Blue moon**

6. Rain on the planet Venus is not water but what very caustic substance?   **A: Sulfuric acid**

7. What cosmic activity is defined as "a sudden, intense variation in brightness which occurs when magnetic energy from sun's atmosphere is released"?   **A: Solar flare**

8. What name is assigned to the brightest star in each constellation (followed by the constellation's name)?   **A: Alpha**

9. What were Soviet astronauts called?   **A: Cosmonauts**

10. What is the term for the theory that the universe was created from the explosion of a mass of hydrogen atoms, recently endorsed by the Pope?   **A: Big bang theory**

11. What northernmost constellation, nicknamed the Little Dipper, contains Polaris at the end of the handle?   **A: Ursa Minor**

12. What is the Latin name of the Dog Star, the brightest star in the sky?   **A: Sirius**

13. What was the first planet in our solar system to be discovered by mathematics?   **A: Neptune**

14. What star-like object emits powerful blue light and often radio waves?   **A: Quasar**

15. What astrological band is divided into 12 equal parts called signs, each bearing the name of a constellation for which it was originally named?   **A: Zodiac**

16. What is the term for the death explosion of a massive star whose core has completely burned out?   **A: Supernova**

17. What constellation in the Southern Hemisphere contains the Dog Star, Sirius?   **A: Canis Major**

18. Name the two known planets in our solar system that have no moons.   **A: Mercury and Venus**

19. What is the term for the scientific study of the positions, distribution, motion and composition of celestial bodies?   **A: Astronomy**

20. What "W" shaped constellation is located in the Northern Hemisphere?   **A: Cassiopeia**

21. What large comet was visible to the naked eye for a record 18 months in 1996 and 1997?   **A: Hale-Bopp**

22. The brightest stars of this constellation in the equatorial region of the sky are Rigel and Betelgeuse.   **A: Orion**

23. What celestial body influences Earth's ocean tides and the lengthening of the day?   **A: Moon**

24. What unit of measurement, roughly the distance from the Earth to the Sun, is used primarily to measure distances within the Solar System?   **A: Astronomical unit**

25. What constellation is in the shape of a dipper with Polaris at the tip of its handle?   **A: Ursa Minor**

26. What was the name of the first artificial Earth satellite?

A: Sputnik

27. What is the proper term for a solid piece of comet or asteroid debris that has fallen to the earth's surface from outer space?

A: Meteorite

28. What government agency received a $400 fine for littering from a small town in Australia when Skylab fell to earth in 1979?   **A: NASA**

29. What planet orbits the sun in 116 days, the fastest speed of all the planets?   **A: Mercury**

30. What rotating neutron stars emit short bursts of radio waves?   **A: Pulsars**

31. What part of the Sun's atmosphere extends outward for several times the Sun's radius and consists of extremely hot plasma which may exceed one million degrees Celsius?   **A: Corona**

32. What natural phenomenon occurs when the Moon enters the

Earth's shadow as the Earth moves between the Sun and the Moon?   **A: Lunar eclipse**

33. This bright spot sometimes appears on either side of the sun and is often called a sundog.   **A: Parhelion**

34. What U.S. astronomer – for whom a telescope is named – was the first to offer evidence to support the theory of the expanding universe?   **A: Edwin Hubble**

35. What Italian physicist and astronomer was tried and sentenced to house arrest by the Roman Inquisition in 1632 for his belief that the Earth orbited the Sun?   **A: Galileo**

36. The name of these dark basaltic plains on the moon comes from the Latin word for sea.   **A: Mare**

37. What private astronomical observatory northeast of San Diego contains the famous 200-inch Hale Telescope?

A: (Mount) Palomar Observatory

38. What is the term for any star that is cool, faint, and small?

A: Red dwarf

39. What constellation represents the twins Castor and Pollux who sailed with the Argonauts in search of the golden fleece?

A: Gemini

40. These cosmic snowballs of frozen gases, rock and dust are about the size of a small town.   **A: Comets**

BUSINESS AND ADVERTISING

1. One can view the Harley-Davidson Museum in this Midwestern city where the first Harley was made.   **A: Milwaukee**

2. Elsa Miranda was the most memorable voice of this fruit company mascot.   **A: Chiquita Brands International**

3. What company's slogan is "Melts in your mouth, not in your hand"?   **A: M & Ms**

4. This company was the first to advertise undergarments on TV in 1955 and the first to show a woman wearing only a bra from the waist up in a 1977 commercial.   **A: Playtex**

5. This fast food restaurant chain which originated in Georgia never opens its doors on Sundays.   **A: Chick-fil-A**

6. What personal computer designed by Apple was named after Steve Jobs' daughter?   **A: The Lisa**

7. What beer was known as "The beer that made Milwaukee famous"?   **A: Schlitz**

8. What is the name of the finicky orange tabby in commercials for Nine Lives?   **A: Morris**

9. What company's first ad slogan "It floats!" was followed by "99 $^{44}/_{100}$% Pure"?   **A: Ivory soap**

10. What company's 3-note chimes were the first audio trademark to be accepted by the U.S. Patent and Trademark Office.

A: NBC

11. What large athletic shoe and apparel corporation takes its name from the Greek goddess of victory?   **A: Nike**

12. What hair styling products company's ad slogan was "A little dab'll do ya"?   **A: Brylcreem**

13. What corporation's long-running ad jingle is "Everybody doesn't like something, but nobody doesn't like _____

_____"?   **A: Sara Lee**

14. What laundry detergent had the catchphrase "ring around the collar"?   **A: Wisk**

15. "Quality is Job 1" was the advertising slogan of this automobile manufacturer.   **A: Ford Motor Company**

16. What company's ad slogan was "Leave the driving to us"?

A: Greyhound

17. What Proctor & Gamble subsidiary's slogan was "Look ma, no cavities!"?   **A: Crest**

18. 83-year-old Clara Peller asked "Where's the beef?" in a commercial for this company.   **A: Wendy's**

19. Pitchmen for this winery said "Thank you for your support" in commercials.   **A: Bartles and Jaymes**

20. What type of bird is Sam, the cartoon character on the Fruit Loops box?   **A: Toucan**

21. The original slogan for this powdered cleanser was "Stronger than dirt," a reference to the muscular hero from Greek mythology.   **A: Ajax**

22. What company holds a "bake-off" every year with the grand prize of 1 million dollars?   **A: Pillsbury**

23. What "spokesfish" has long been the cartoon mascot for the StarKist brand of tuna?   **A: Charlie the Tuna**

24. What soft drink was the beverage of choice for Forrest Gump in his namesake movie?   **A: Dr. Pepper**

25. In 2008, the slogan of this product was, "Drink it slow. Doctor's orders."   **A: Dr. Pepper**

26. What is the term for an agreement between competing private companies to fix prices or control competition?   **A: Cartel**

27. To what did S. S. Kresge Corporation change its name in 1977?   **A: Kmart Corporation**

28. What fictional character, along with his mule Conchita, advertises 100% Colombian coffee beans?   **A: Juan Valdez**

29. What cigarette was successfully marketed as tasting good "like a cigarette should."   **A: Winston**

30. What type of shopping outlet consists of a row of businesses that usually open onto a common parking lot?   **A: Strip mall**

31. What soap, the world's best-selling soap at the start of the 20th century, was named for the two oils it contained?   **A: Palmolive**

32. What video game, the first released by Atari, featured a simulated table-tennis game?   **A: Pong**

33. What is the U.S. equivalent of an "ironmonger" store in Great Britain?   **A: Hardware store**

34. What is the term for a strike which is called without official union authorization?   **A: Wildcat strike**

35. What is the term for a business employing both union and non-union workers?   **A: Open shop**

36. What was the first fast food chain?   **A: White Castle**

37. The slogan "When you care enough to send the very best" belongs to this company, the largest manufacturer of greeting cards in the U.S.   **A: Hallmark**

38. What Michigan city is home to Kellogg Company, Post Cereals and a Ralston Foods cereal factory?   **A: Battle Creek**

39. What is the term for a workplace with unacceptable working conditions, including poor pay, long hours or use of child labor?   **A: Sweatshop**

40. What London store with 330 departments is one of the world's most famous stores?   **A: Harrods**

41. In one of its most famous ads, Orson Welles declared "We will sell no wine before its time," for this company.   **A: Paul Masson**

42. What corn chip mascot with oversized yellow hat, crossed bandoliers and a handlebar mustache was retired with pressure from the National Mexican-American Anti-Defamation Committee?   **A: Frito Bandito**

43. What product was Hormel Company of Austin, Minnesota, introduced to the world in 1937 by Hormel Company of Austin, Minnesota?   **A: Spam**

44. "When it rains, it pours" is the advertising slogan for what company?   **A: Morton Salt**

45. The Coca-Cola ad song "I'd Like to Buy the World a Coke" by The New Seekers was reworked as what song to become a top ten hit for the group in 1972?   **A: I'd Like to Teach the World to Sing**

46. What supermarket chain was the largest food retailer in the U.S. from 1915 through 1975?   **A: A & P (The Great Atlantic and Pacific Tea Company)**

47. What Mattel doll was introduced in 1963 as Barbie's best friend to counteract criticism that Barbie was a sex symbol?   **A: Midge**

48. What soft-serve franchise sells the "Blizzard"?   **A: Dairy Queen**

49. December, 1970 was the last time a commercial advertising this product was aired on U.S. TV.   **A: Cigarettes**

50. What statuette, named after the Muse of history, is awarded annually for outstanding achievement in radio and television advertising?   **A: Clio**

CLASSICAL MUSIC

1. What Polish-born composer who wrote "Heroic Polonaise in A flat *major* Op. 53" was often called "The Poet of the Piano"?

A: **Frédéric Chopin**

2. Mozart composed twelve variations of this tune, formerly a French folk song but now used for several children's songs.

A: **"Twinkle Twinkle Little Star"**

3. In the U.S., major ballet companies generate around 40% of their annual ticket revenues from performances of what two-act ballet by Tchaikovsky?   A: **"The Nutcracker"**

4. What does the word "fine" on a piece of sheet music indicate?

A: **The end**

5. What composer was crowned "The Waltz King?"   A: **Johann Strauss II**

6. What 20th century Russian composer shocked audiences with his 1913 avant-garde work "Rite of Spring"?   A: **Igor Stravinsky**

7. What American composer was nicknamed "The March King"?

A: **John Philip Sousa**

8. Which of Beethoven's symphonies starts off with four now-famous distinctive notes?   A: **Fifth Symphony or "Symphony No. 5"**

9. What Tchaikovsky ballet tells the story of Odette, a princess

turned into a swan by an evil sorcerer's curse?   **A: "Swan Lake"**

10. What is the proper term for the introductory instrumental music for an opera, ballet or oratorio?   **A: Overture**

11. What German composer had his own opera house built where his four-opera cycle "Der Ring des Nibelungen" was performed?

A: Richard Wagner

12. What is the term for a piece for one voice usually found in an opera, oratorio or cantata?   **A: Aria**

13. What is the term for a somber musical piece performed at a funeral or memorial service?   **A: Dirge**

14. What famous oratorio by George Frideric Handel contains his "Hallelujah" chorus?   **A: Messiah**

15. What Giacomo Puccini opera is set in 1800 Rome threatened by Napoleon's invasion of Italy?   **A: "Tosca"**

16. What 1936 Sergei Prokofiev composition is a children's story about a boy's encounter with a wolf?   **A: "Peter and the Wolf"**

17. What is the musical term for the decoration of an operatic melody with elaborate trills and runs?   **A: Coloratura**

18. What Georges Bizet opera tells the story of the seduction of naïve soldier Don Jose by a fickle gypsy?   **A: "Carmen"**

19. Who composed the Baroque era instrumental works "The Brandenburg Concertos"?   **A: Johann Sebastian Bach**

20. What world-renowned opera house opened in Milan in 1778?

   A: La Scala

21. These orchestra drums, also called kettledrums, evolved from military drums.   **A: Timpani**

22. What term for a flute player was first used by Nathaniel Hawthorne in his 1860 book "The Marble Faun"?   **A: Flautist**

23. Although this French composer is most noted for "Prelude, Afternoon of a Faun," he also composed "Clair de Lune." **A: Claude Debussy**

24. What German composer's works include "Till Eulenspiegel," "Thus Spake Zarathustra," and "Salome"?   **A: Richard Strauss**

CLOTHING AND TEXTILES

1. Abraham Lincoln wore this type of tall silk hat named for its resemblance to a rooftop fixture.   **A: Stovepipe hat**

2. What pattern of abstract, curved shapes originated from a town in Scotland famous for its textiles?   **A: Paisley**

3. What weaving term refers to the vertical threads attached to the top and bottom of a loom through which the weft is woven?

A: Warp

4. What whimsically-named coarse wool fabric is woven from linen warp and coarse wool filling?   **A: Linsey-woolsey**

5. What is another name for the yarn made from the hair of the angora goat?   **A: Mohair**

6. The sneakers introduced to America in 1916 by U.S. Rubber were originally called what?   **A: Keds**

7. What British fashion designer is credited with creating the miniskirt in 1964?   **A: Mary Quant**

8. This medium-weight, plain weave fabric used for shirts and curtains usually has a check pattern.   **A: Gingham**

9. What is the proper term for a skullcap worn by Jewish men and boys?   **A: Yarmulke**

10. This heavy jacquard-type fabric, used for upholstery, draperies and formal wear, has an all-over raised pattern or floral design.

A: Brocade

11. What small cap with a flat crown and straight sides was made popular in the early 1960s by Jackie Kennedy?   **A: Pillbox**

12. What sturdy cloth's name is derived from the French term "serge de Nîmes" where the fabric originated?   **A: Denim**

13. The lush, dark brown fur of the Russian marten is called this.   **A: Sable**

14. What lightweight cotton fabric with a striped, plaid or checked pattern that bleeds when washed is usually imported from India?   **A: Madras**

15. What is the term for a straw hat woven from leaves of the jipijapa plant of Central and South America?   **A: Panama hat**

16. What ancient fabric is made from the fibers of the woody stem of the flax plant?   **A: Linen**

17. The name of this thick, coarse fabric used to make durable work clothes is also another word for blue jeans.   **A: Dungaree(s)**

18. What broad pleated waist sash which originally was worn by tribal warriors in Afghanistan is now mainly worn with a tuxedo?

A: Cummerbund

19. This fiber from India is used for gunny sacks, bags, cordage and binding threads in carpets and rugs.   **A: Jute**

20. What is the term for the fur pouch often worn with a kilt by Scottish men?   **A: Sporran**

21. What short double-breasted coat of heavy woolen material (usually plaid) is named after a city in Michigan?   **A: Mackinaw**

22. This rough, coarse cloth was chiefly worn as a symbol of

penitence or mourning.   **A: Sackcloth**

23. This three-cornered hat or "cocked hat" was popular in Revolutionary War days.   **A: Tricorne or tricorn**

24. What kind of socks are knit with a diamond-shaped pattern on a solid background?   **A: Argyle**

25. What is the term for the leather shorts worn with suspenders worn especially in Bavaria?   **A: Lederhosen**

COMICS AND CARTOONS

1. What kind of airplane did Snoopy fly in battles with his arch-enemy the Red Baron?   **A: Sopwith Camel**

2. For which Metropolis newspaper did Superman's alter ego Clark Kent work?   **A: Daily Planet**

3. What moviemaker won 22 Academy Awards (from 59 nominations) and four honorary Academy Awards, giving him more awards and nominations than any other person in history?

A: Walt Disney

4. What is the nearsighted Mr. Magoo's first name?   **A: Quincy**

5. What blue dog's show featured Jellystone Park and Yogi Bear?

A: Huckleberry Hound

6. What was the favorite exclamation of the title character in the comic strip "Little Orphan Annie"?   **A: Leapin Lizards!**

7. What pen name was used by Alfred Gerald Caplin, the creator of "Li'l Abner,"?   **A: Al Capp**

8. What voice actor provided the voice of Bugs Bunny, Daffy Duck and Elmer Fudd?   **A: Mel Blanc**

9. What was the name of the Flintstones family pet?   **A: Dino**

10. What cartoon strip featuring social and political commentary was the first to ever win a Pulitzer Prize?   **A: Doonesbury**

11. What color took away the awesome power of early versions of The Green Lantern?   **A: yellow**

12. What comic strip featured a bowling-pin shaped animal called a shmoo that gave milk and laid eggs?   **A: Lil Abner**

13. Tess Trueheart was the wife of what Chester Gould comic strip character?   **A: Dick Tracy**

14. What cat was the star of the first major x-rated cartoon?

A: Fritz the Cat

15. What was the appropriate name of the horse-ghost buddy of Casper, the Friendly Ghost?   **A: Nightmare**

16. What comic strip character's name (from the cartoon series "The Timid Soul") has become synonymous with a timid, meek or unassertive person?   **A: Caspar Milquetoast**

17. What "Popeye" character had the famous catchphrase ""I'll gladly pay you Tuesday for a hamburger today"?   **A: Wimpy**

18. Olive Oyl's measurements consisted of all what number?

A: 19-19-19

19. Who was Popeye's original (pre-1960) muscular, bearded archenemy?   **A: Bluto**

20. With what jewelry items does Wonder Woman deflect bullets?   **A: Golden bracelets**

21. What was the name of the Flintstones' home town?

A: Bedrock

22. What cartoonist invented the cartoon strip "Blondie" and its "Dagwood sandwich"?   **A: Chic Young**

23. Mort Walker created this cartoon strip set on a U.S. Army post in 1950.   **A: Beetle Bailey**

24. The ingredients of this volatile brew from "Li'l Abner" are still a mystery.   **A: Kickapoo Joy Juice**

25. What cartoon character used complex contraptions to try to catch the Road Runner?   **A: Wile E. Coyote**

CUSTOMS

1. In India, what part of a Hindu elder's body would you touch to show your respect?   **A: Feet**

2. In Greece, this day is the unlucky day of the week instead of Friday when it falls on the 13th.   **A: Tuesday**

3. What is the loose, skirt-like loincloth which men in the rural areas of India wear?   **A: Dhoti**

4. What carved objects represented the kinship system of a clan and were an important part of the coastal First Nations Potlatch ceremony?   **A: Totem poles**

5. What national symbol of Ireland was first used by St. Patrick to represent the Trinity?   **A: Shamrock**

6. It is customary for women to give men this item on Valentine's Day in Japan.   **A: Chocolate**

7. What flirtatious American practice is considered to be rude to women in Australia?   **A: Winking**

8. What is the term for a custom or belief shared by the members of a group as part of their common culture?   **A: Folkway**

9. What number do Japanese people consider unlucky, since it is similar to the word for death?   **A: Four**

10. In some highland tribes in this Melanesian country, it is customary for men to greet each other by rubbing each other's groin regions.   **A: Papua New Guinea**

11. What is the Spanish term for a 15th birthday ceremony which marks a girl's passage to womanhood?   **A: Quinceanera**

12. What custom originated in ancient times when strangers did it to show that they held no weapons?   **A: Handshake**

13. Women in this country do not celebrate their 30th birthdays because 30 is considered a year of danger and uncertainty.

A: China

14. In China, these food items are traditionally eaten on birthdays because they symbolize long life.   **A: Long noodles**

15. In the Middle Ages, people took their names from their occupations, such as Chandler. What was Webster's occupation?

A: Weaving

16. In this Mediterranean country, people celebrate the "name day" of the saint that bears their name rather than their own birthday.   **A: Greece**

17. Women in this European country dress in black for up to a year following a death and men wear black armbands for up to 40 days.

A: Greece

18. This term for departing without notice or permission originated in 18th century France when it was the custom to depart from a social occasion without formally bidding the host goodbye.

A: French leave

19. What gelatinous pork product is considered to be a classy gift for the Lunar New Year in South Korea?   **A: Spam**

20. What now-outlawed practice allowed Polynesians to destroy the "mana" or power of their opponents? **A: Cannibalism**

21. What is the term for a significant event, usually marked by ceremony, that indicates a transition from one stage of life to another?   **A: Rite of passage**

22. To prevent bad luck, these Scandinavians knock on wood while reciting "Peppar, peppar ta i trä" ("Pepper, pepper touch wood.")

A: Swedes

23. Because it is a Shinto country rather than Christian, reading a pornographic magazine in public is not considered rude here.

A: Japan

24. On what side of the road does one drive in Japan?   **A: Left**

25. In this country it is strongly forbidden to say "cheers" or "Prost" with water, because you are literally wishing death to all your drinking buddies.   **A: Germany**

EXPLORERS

1. What explorer sailed around the Pacific Ocean for 12 years, encountering the Sandwich Islands for the first time and claiming Australia's east coast for Britain? **A: Captain James Cook**

2. What explorer died of dysentery in 1596 – not long after losing the Battle of San Juan – and was buried in full armor in a lead coffin near Portobelo, Panama? **A: Sir Francis Drake**

3. What underwater researcher co-developed the Aqua-Lung?

A: Jacques Cousteau

4. Who was the first person to reach the South Pole? **A: Roald Amundsen**

5. What luxury car was named for the French adventurer who founded the city of Detroit? **A: Cadillac**

6. Roald Amundsen, the first man to reach the South Pole, was a citizen of what country? **A: Norway**

7. What Spanish explorer was the first European to reach the Pacific Ocean from the New World? **A: Vasco Núñez de Balboa**

8. What English mountaineer's body was found at 27,000 feet on the north face of Mount Everest, 75 years after his summit attempt? **A: George Mallory**

9. What 19th century Scottish Congregationalist missionary to Africa failed in his search for the source of the Nile? **A: David Livingstone**

10. What Spanish conquistador overthrew the Aztec rulers of Mexico in the 1500s and brought Mexico under the authority of Spain?

A: Hernán Cortés

11. What Jesuit missionary explored the Mississippi River for France in 1673?   **A: Fr. Jacques Marquette**

12. What Florentine explorer, for whom a bridge in New York Harbor is named, was the first European to explore the Atlantic coast of North America?   **A: Giovanni da Verrazzano**

13. What Portuguese explorer was the first European to reach India by sea, establishing an all-water route from Europe to Asia?

A: Vasco da Gama

14. What English baron founded the colony of Maryland as a haven for Catholics in the New World?   **A: Cecil Calvert, 2nd Baron Baltimore (Lord Baltimore)**

15. What Genoese explorer thought he had reached the East Indies in 1492 but instead landed on a Bahamian island he named San Salvador?   **A: Christopher Columbus**

16. What American explorer came within 60 miles of the geographic North Pole in 1909?   **A: Robert Edwin Peary, Sr.**

17. What Italian merchant wrote a book in 1300 about his travels to Central Asia and China, introducing Europeans to those countries for the first time?   **A: Marco Polo**

18. What John Denver song was written as a tribute to Jacques-Yves Cousteau and his research ship?   **A: Calypso**

19. What name did Dutch explorer Abel Tasman apply to what is now Australia when he mapped its coast in 1644?   **A: New Holland**

20. What U.S. president commissioned Captain Meriwether Lewis and Second Lieutenant William Clark to explore the newly acquired Louisiana Purchase?   **A: Thomas Jefferson**

FOOD

1. There are 7500 known cultivars of this pomaceous fruit of the malus domestica tree.   **A: Apple**

2. Bay leaves, formerly used to crown winning athletes, today flavor meats and stews. From what tree do they come?   **A: Laurel**

3. What substance can be added to boiling water to keep your pasta from sticking together?   **A: Oil**

4. What process involving quick heating and cooling is used to kill harmful microorganisms in milk?   **A: Pasteurization**

5. Garlic bulbs are divided into fleshy sections called what?

A: Cloves

6. What anti-caking agent is added to confectioner's sugar?

A: Corn starch

7. The dominant term in America and Canada for this condiment is "ketchup" but some southern states still call it this.   **A: Catsup**

8. In what country did "Tapas," a type of hors d' oeuvre, originate?

A: Spain

9. What national dish of Scotland is the heart, liver, lungs and small intestine of a calf or sheep boiled in the stomach of the animal?

A: Haggis

10. These berries used to flavor wild game are actually fleshy conifer cones.   **A: Juniper berries**

11. The expensive spice of saffron comes from what spring corm?

A: Crocus

12. What salad dressing of mayonnaise seasoned with pickles, pimientos and sweet peppers is named after a location in the St. Lawrence River?　**A: Thousand Island**

13. What is the French term for a spreadable liver paste made from specially fattened geese or ducks?　**A: Pate**

14. What is the proper term for vegetables cut into thin strips which are used for garnishing?　**A: Julienne**

15. Hippomenes threw three of these golden fruits to distract Atalanta so that he could win the race and her hand.　**A: Apples**

16. The milk of what breed of cow generally yields the highest percentage of milk fat?　**A: Jersey (5.2%)**

17. A highly respected job title in Japan is that of "Tōji," or brewer of this fermented rice wine.　**A: Sake or saki**

18. The highest grade of tea leaf in the tea industry is referred to as this.　**A: Orange pekoe**

19. Parts of this second-most poisonous vertebrate in the world are a delicacy in Japan, China and Korea when prepared by a specially-trained seafood chef.　**A: Pufferfish**

20. What chocolate cookie with a sweet cream filling has become the best-selling brand of cookie in the U.S.?　**A: Oreo**

21. What is the term for a buffet-style Scandinavian meal serving a variety of hot and cold dishes?　**A: Smorgasbord**

22. What type of ice cream which originated in Italy consists of blocks of vanilla, chocolate and strawberry molded together?
A: Neapolitan

23. What sweet dessert made of layers of flaky pastry filled with nuts and sugar and brushed with honey originated in the Ottoman Empire?　**A: Baklava**

24. What food item must be offered at every meal if a U.S. school district wishes to get reimbursement from the federal government?

A: Milk

25. What rich soup from Eastern Europe usually contains beets?

A: Borscht

26. This former "food of the gods" on Mt. Olympus now designates a dessert of chilled fruit (usually bananas and oranges) mixed with coconut.　**A: Ambrosia**

27. What sweet flaky pastry has jam or fruit folded into it?

A: Danish

28. What traditional Norwegian fish dish consists of dried cod cured in lye then reconstituted by boiling?　**A: Lutefisk**

29. What is the Scottish name for smoked haddock?　**A: Finnan haddie**

30. What is the Italian word for squid?　**A: Calamari**

31. What is the culinary term for the thymus gland of an animal – usually lamb or veal?　**A: Sweetbread**

32. Meat is never added to make an authentic version of this Italian vegetable soup made with beans and pasta or rice. **A: Minestrone**

33. What cooking oil – also called "Canada Oil" – is produced from a strain of the rapeseed plant?　**A: Canola oil**

34. What spice commonly used in Indian cooking is actually a blend of turmeric, chili powder, coriander, cumin, ginger and pepper?

A: **Curry powder**

35. "Haricots verts" is the French phrase for what vegetable?

A: **Green beans**

36. What food is advertised as "The San Francisco Treat"?

A: **Rice-A-Roni**

37. What excellent source of protein made from processed soy beans is also called "bean curd"?   A: **Tofu**

38. What spice traditionally used to flavor "stuffing" comes from the evergreen, woody-stemmed "salvia officinalis" shrub?   A: **Sage**

39. What term is used to describe the aroma of wine?   A: **Bouquet**

40. What steamed rice dish contains bits of vegetables, shellfish or meat?   A: **Rice pilaf**

41. What soup of southern U.S.A. origin is traditionally thickened with okra pods?   A: **Gumbo**

42. What color is the "Granny Smith" apple popular in apple pies?

A: **Green**

43. What is the culinary term for ground spiced chickpeas formed into balls and fried?   A: **Felafel**

44. What is the term for the cultivation of fish and shellfish for food?   A: **Aquaculture**

45. What cocktail is made of sweet vermouth and whiskey?

A: **Manhattan**

46. What brand of syrup was created by a Minnesota grocer in 1887 in honor of Abraham Lincoln's boyhood home?   **A: Log Cabin**

47. What confection is made of nuts stirred in boiling sugar syrup?

A: Praline

48. What is the term for poultry or meat cut up and stewed in gravy?

A: Fricassee

49. What type of caviar comes from a large white sturgeon?

A: Beluga

50. What great conqueror brought dwarfed apples, the forerunners of today's dwarfing rootstocks, from Kazakhstan back to Macedonia in 328 BCE?   **A: Alexander the Great**

FOREIGN AFFAIRS

1. What common legal process did Italy finally legalize in December of 1970?   **A: Divorce**

2. What is the name of the British government department which collects taxes and manages revenues?   **A: Exchequer**

3. What European country obtains the highest percentage of its electricity from nuclear power with 75%?   **A: France**

4. What multilateral agreement regulating international trade was created in 1995 as a successor to the General Agreement on Tariffs and Trade?   **A: World Trade Organization**

5. The two non-member "observer" states of the United Nations General Assembly are Palestine and this one.   **A: Holy See (Vatican City)**

6. What is the term for the systematic elimination of an ethnic or religious group from a region or society, i.e. Hitler's "final solution"?
A: Ethnic cleansing

7. What term is used to describe any of several small, politically-unstable nations in Latin America that have economies based on a few agricultural crops?   **A: Banana republics**

8. All the Nobel Prizes except for the Peace Prize are awarded in what city each year?   **A: Stockholm**

9. Which of the two houses of the British Parliament is the most powerful (because its ruling party leader is the Prime Minister of Britain)?   **A: House of Commons**

10. What legal holiday in Canada, formerly called Dominion Day, is the anniversary of the country's formation in 1867?   **A: Canada Day**

11. What form of government can be found in Japan today?

A: Constitutional monarchy

12. What French president used his veto power to stop UK attempts to join the European Union (formerly European Communities) from 1961 to 1969 because he viewed British membership as a Trojan horse for U.S. influence?   **A: Charles De Gaulle**

13. What is the term for the surrender and delivery of a foreign criminal to the authorities in his homeland?   **A: Extradition**

14. What country in 1893 became the first country to grant all of its adult female citizens the right to vote?   **A: New Zealand**

15. What international treaty made the continent of Antarctica off-limits to oil drilling until 2048?   **A: Madrid Protocol (Protocol on Environmental Protection to the Antarctic Treaty)**

16. What surname did Queen Elizabeth II officially declare in 1960 as the official surname of her direct descendants?   **A: Mountbatten-Windsor**

17. What term was originally applied to Afghani freedom fighters but now applies to any radical Muslim militant groups?

A: Mujahideen

18. Albert Lutuli, President of the African National Congress was the first anti-apartheid worker to receive the Nobel Peace Prize (1960). Who was the second?   **A: Bishop Desmond Tutu**

19. What is the term for diplomatic negotiations conducted by an official intermediary who travels frequently between the nations involved?   **A: Shuttle diplomacy**

20. The Mau Mau were a secret guerrilla movement in this country between 1952 and 1960.   **A: Kenya**

21. Who is the titular head of the Commonwealth of Nations (formerly the British Commonwealth)?   **A: Queen Elizabeth II**

22. What word is a metonym for the British governmental administration or civil service?   **A: Whitehall**

23. What is the term for a person, usually a skilled professional, temporarily or permanently residing in a country other than that of the person's birth?   **A: Expatriate**

24. There are five countries that have a Communist politburo, or executive committee for a political party, today: China, North Korea, Laos, Vietnam and this one.   **A: Cuba**

25. What is the term for an international conference of the highest-ranking government officials?   **A: Summit**

GAMES, HOBBIES AND PASTIMES

1. In the game of Hearts, this tactic is used to try to obtain the highest possible outcome through the risky strategy of achieving the lowest possible score.   **A: Shooting the moon**

2. In the game of cribbage, the player who scores 30 points or less to the winner's 61 is said to be in this losing position.   **A: Lurch**

3. What board game took its name from the old English reflecting the strategy of "sending back" pieces to the board?   **A: Backgammon**

4. A "kegler" is a person who enjoys this pastime.   **A: Bowling**

5. What chalk-on-pavement game is called "Potsy" in New York City?   **A: Hopscotch**

6. In what popular card game are players identified by cardinal directions such as "north"?   **A: Contract bridge**

7. In this table game, each side of the board has a track of 12 long triangles, called points.   **A: Backgammon**

8. What dice game evolved from earlier dice games such as Yacht, Generala, and Yogi?   **A: Yahtzee**

9. Any time a pinochle player accidentally misplays during the play portion of the hand it is called this.   **A: Renege**

10. Eight-ball is the most widely played pocket pool game, but professional pool players generally play this game.   **A: Nine-ball**

11. What card game which introduced the joker to modern decks was considered the national card game of the 19th century?

A: Euchre

12. Possible murder sites in this board game include the library, the billiard room and the conservatory. **A: Clue**

13. What simulated table tennis game introduced in the early 1970s was one of the first to reach mainstream popularity? **A: Pong**

14. What is the highest possible hand value in the casino card game baccarat? **A: 9**

15. What is the Japanese art of folding squares of paper into representational shapes? **A: Origami**

16. The Japanese art of flower arranging is called what? **A: Ikebana**

17. On what Asian island were yoyos originally used as weapons, with sharp edges and studs attached to 20-foot ropes for flinging at prey? **A: Philippines**

18. "The League of Ordinary Gentlemen" was a 2006 documentary featuring four PBA tour players in this sport. **A: Bowling**

19. What sport played a pivotal role in the popular 1998 film "The Big Lebowski"? **A: Bowling**

20. Roman legionaries tossing stone objects as close as possible to other stone objects around 2,000 years ago eventually evolved into what Italian game? **A: Bocce**

21. In bowling, three consecutive strikes are known as this.

A: Turkey

22. What is the British name for tic-tac-toe?   **A: Noughts and crosses**

23. The rest of the U.S. calls it 'gambling,' but what is it called in Nevada?   **A: Gaming**

24. What game is believed to have originated in Eastern India where its early pieces represented infantry, cavalry, elephants and chariotry?   **A: Chess**

25. What game is played with a set of 144 tiles based on Chinese characters and symbols?   **A: Mah jongg**

GEOGRAPHY

1. In what country is the Waterloo battlefield where Napoleon was defeated?　**A: Belgium**

2. What river is the widest river in the world?　**A: Amazon**

3. Tiananmen Square, the scene of 1989 pro-democracy protests, is located in which Chinese city?　**A: Beijing**

4. This state claims to produce 90% of the world's toothpick supply.　**A: Maine**

5. What Canadian province's historic ties to Scotland are symbolized by a red lion on its flag?　**A: Nova Scotia**

6. What is the only Canadian province that borders the Pacific Ocean?　**A: British Columbia**

7. The name of what city means "protected bay" in Hawaiian?
A: Honolulu

8. What Southeast Asian country's most populous city and federal capital is Kuala Lumpur?　**A: Malaysia**

9. What 14th-century cathedral is situated on the French Ile de la Cite, an island in the Seine?　**A: Notre Dame**

10. What Alpine peak, at nearly 16,000 feet, is the highest mountain in Europe?　**A: Mount Blanc**

11. The source of what American river can be found in Lake Itasca in Northern Minnesota?　**A: Mississippi**

12. Which American city, like Rome, was built on seven hills?

A: Seattle

13. What islands located in the northern part of the Lesser Antilles were named for the unmarried Queen Elizabeth I?   A: Virgin Islands

14. What country resulted from the union of Tanganyika and Zanzibar? A: Tanzania

15. What ancient country, under five centuries of Roman control after the birth of Christ, encompassed present day France, Luxembourg, Belgium and parts of Switzerland, Northern Italy, Netherlands and Germany?   A: Gaul

16. What was the only airport to serve Paris before the construction of Charles de Gaulle Airport in 1974?   A: Orly

17. What Southeast Asian country was known as Siam until 1939?

A: Thailand

18. What river, Europe's second longest, originates in the Black Forest of Germany and empties into the Black Sea?   A: Danube

19. What is the name of the body of water that separates Russia from the U.S.?   A: The Bering Strait

20. What mountain range in Northeastern Italy was named after the French mineralogist Déodat Gratet de Dolomieu?   A: Dolomites

21. What 115-island country in the Indian Ocean has the smallest population of any African state with 90,024 inhabitants?

A: Seychelles

22. What Scottish village became famous for "runaway marriages" because it was the first easily reachable village over the Scottish border from England?   **A: Gretna Green**

23. In what country is the bridge over the river Kwai, the site of the construction of the "Death Railway" by British prisoners of war?

A: Myanmar (Burma)

24. Guadalcanal of W. W. II fame is part of what Pacific Island group?   **A: The Solomons**

25. What is the name of the hydrological feature that separates the watersheds that drain into the Atlantic Ocean from those that drain into the Pacific?   **A: Continental or Great Divide**

26. What park, Canada's oldest national park, encompasses 2,564 square miles west of Calgary, Alberta?   **A: Banff National Park**

27. What is Ukraine's largest and richest city?   **A: Kiev (Kyiv)**

28. What country, the world's largest archipelago, consists of 17,508 islands scattered over both sides of the equator in the Indian Ocean?   **A: Indonesia**

29. What country in Southeast Europe changed its name in 2003 to Serbia and Montenegro?   **A: Yugoslavia**

30. Contrary to popular belief, this Florida city's name doesn't mean "rat's mouth" but instead refers to "a shallow inlet of sharp-pointed rocks which scrapes a ship's cables."   **A: Boca Raton**

31. In what African country is Mount Kilimanjaro, the highest free-standing mountain in the world?   **A: Tanzania**

32. Today this name no longer refers to the University of Paris but to the historical building which housed it, located in Paris's Latin Quarter on the left bank of the Seine.   **A: Sorbonne**

33. The name of this resort/boardwalk area in the Southwestern part of the borough of Brooklyn, N.Y. means "Rabbit Island." **A: Coney Island**

34. Seventy percent of the population of the Bahamas lives in this city, its capital.   **A: Nassau**

35. What softly rolling, grassy plains cover the greater part of eastern Argentina?   **A: Pampas**

36. How does one refer to a native of Monaco?   **A: Monegasque**

37. What was the name of the Kolkata (Calcutta), India airport before being renamed after Netaji Subhas Chandra Bose, a prominent leader of Indian independence movement?   **A: Dum Dum Airport**

38. The driest nonpolar desert in the world is a 600-mile long plateau in Chile. What is its name?   **A: Atacama Desert**

39. What line divides the globe into the Western and Eastern hemispheres?   **A: Prime Meridian**

40. The Alpine region of Tyrol be found in what European country? **A: Austria**

41. The indigenous Inuit people who inhabit this country's Western region call it Kalaallit Nunaat (land of the Kalaallit).   **A: Greenland**

42. What national park in Alaska's interior was renamed "Denali National Park and Preserve" in 1980?   **A: Mount McKinley**

43. What range of the Appalachians gets its name from the isoprene released into the atmosphere by its trees?   **A: Blue Ridge Mountains**

44. What American Southwest's city's name means "the meadows" in Spanish?   **A: Las Vegas**

45. What famous promontory on the Southeast coast of Oahu is 761' high?   **A: Diamond Head**

46. What West African country was established as a home for former slaves with the assistance of the American Colonization Society?   **A: Liberia**

47. Which section of New York's Manhattan Island, a haven for artists, is named for a borough of London, England?

A: Greenwich Village

48. What large freshwater lake in Northeastern Israel, also called Kinneret, featured prominently in the Gospels of the Bible?

A: Sea of Galilee

49. What city is Japan's biggest seaport and second largest city?

A: Yokohama

50. Aer Lingus is the national flag carrier and oldest airline of what European country?   **A: Ireland**

GEOLOGY

1. The rupture of what geological fault caused the San Francisco earthquake of 1906?   **A: San Andreas fault**

2. On the Mohs scale of mineral hardness, what is the hardest known natural substance?   **A: Diamond**

3. What light, ductile metal is the most abundant metal in the earth's crust?   **A: Aluminum**

4. What is the term for the flat, fan-shaped accumulation of sediment deposited at the mouth of a river or stream?   **A: Delta**

5. What type of rock is formed by cooling and solidification from a molten state, especially from molten magma or lava?   **A: Igneous**

6. What glassy black mineraloid is formed by rapidly cooling lava?   **A: Obsidian**

7. What metal is usually alloyed with copper to form bronze?
A: Tin

8. The area of volcano and earthquake activity in the basin of the Pacific Ocean is called what by geologists?   **A: Ring of fire**

9. What is the term for the very hard, compact variety of coal which burn with a blue, smokeless flame?   **A: Anthracite**

10. Which gemstone is a transparent red variety of the mineral corundum?   **A: Ruby**

11. When a loose rock is more than one foot in diameter, it is called a _____.   **A: Boulder**

12. Fossils are most commonly found in this type of rock because it forms at temperatures and pressures that do not destroy fossil remnants.   **A: Sedimentary**

13. A machine which measures the intensity of earthquakes by recording the waves they generate is called what? **A: Seismograph**

14. One of the most common components of peat is this type of moss.   **A: Sphagnum**

15. What is the term for crude iron cast in blocks?   **A: Pig iron**

16. Florence, Italy is the center of trade today for this translucent or white-tinted gypsum used especially for carving.   **A: Alabaster**

17. What cinder cone volcano first erupted in a corn field in Mexico in 1943 and grew to a final height of 1,391 feet?   **A: Parícutin**

18. The process of applying a protective coat of rust-resistant zinc to iron or steel is called what?   **A: Galvanization**

19. What is the term for a naturally magnetized piece of magnetite?   **A: Lodestone**

20. What Missouri city is the center of the largest system of geological faults in the eastern U.S.?   **A: New Madrid**

21. What is the formal term for fool's gold?   **A: Pyrite**

22. What alloy of tin is used for kitchen utensils and tableware?
A: Pewter

23. What semi-precious gemstone is a blue variety of the mineral beryl?   **A: Aquamarine**

24. The Great Pyramid and its complex in Giza, Egypt are made of this sedimentary rock.   **A: Limestone**

25. What adsorbent mineral substance got its name through its historic use by textile workers for cleaning or "fulling" wool? **A: Fuller's earth**

HOLIDAYS

1. "Babbo Natale" or Father Christmas is this country's version of Santa Claus.   **A: Italy**

2. By what name was Memorial Day known in the United States prior to World War II?   **A: Decoration Day**

3. In Sweden, what saint's day is commemorated on December 13th by young girls wearing evergreen crowns of candles in their hair?   **A: St. Lucia**

4. Charles, Duke of Orleans, sent the first known one of these to his wife in France while he was confined in the Tower of London after the Battle of Agincourt in 1415.   **A: Valentine**

5. "Good morrow! 'Tis St. Valentine's Day / All in the morning betime / And I a maid at the window / To be your valentine" was a line spoken by this Danish noblewoman in "Hamlet."   **A: Ophelia**

6. A successful advertising campaign in the 1970s made eating at this fast food chain around Christmas time a popular national custom in Japan. Reservations are taken months in advance.
A: KFC (Kentucky Fried Chicken)

7. What week-long celebration (December 26 – January 1) in the United States and West African nations honors African-American culture with feasting and gift-giving?   **A: Kwanzaa**

8. Also called bûche de Noël, this chocolate sponge cake filled with raspberry jam is a Christmas tradition in countries with French heritage.   **A: Yule log**

9. What Christian feast is observed on January 6th celebrating the visit of the Magi to Jesus? **A: Epiphany**

10. What legal holiday in Canada, formerly called Dominion Day, is the anniversary of the country's formation in 1867?   **A: Canada Day**

11. What country celebrates Thanksgiving on the second Monday of October?   **A: Canada**

12. What historic masked parade takes place in Philadelphia on New Year's Day?   **A: The Mummer's Parade**

13. What holiday is celebrated every year on the last Friday in April by planting a tree?   **A: Arbor Day**

14. What holiday is commemorated every year on November 11 (along with Remembrance Day and Veterans Day) to mark the cessation of hostilities on the Western Front of WWI?

A: Armistice Day

15. South Dakota bucks national tradition and celebrates this holiday on the second Monday of October as "Native American Day."   **A: Columbus Day**

16. What holiday was the first holiday to be designated by presidential proclamation (1789)?   **A: Thanksgiving**

17. What U.S. holiday has the highest greeting card sales?

A: Christmas

18. Most military bases fire a 13-gun salute at noon on this holiday, one for each state in the original United States.   **A: Independence Day (4th of July)**

19. What novella by Charles Dickens ends with "God bless us one and all"?   **A: A Christmas Carol**

20. The eve of this February 2 holiday was the day in which Christmas greenery was taken down in medieval England.

A: Candlemas

21. This term refers to a ceremonial gift-giving feast practiced by the indigenous peoples of the Pacific Northwest.   **A: Potlatch**

22. What holiday falls on the last day of the year in Scotland and features the practice of "first-footing" (gifting the first person to cross your threshold)?   **A: Hogmanay**

23. What is the term for the two-day Jewish New Year celebrated by the ancient customs of sounding the shofar and eating symbolic foods?   **A: Rosh Hashanah**

24. A major offensive was launched on this holiday, the Vietnamese New Year, during the Vietnam War.   **A: Tet**

25. What holiday dates back to October 12, 1810, when Crown Prince Ludwig of Bavaria invited the entire kingdom to celebrate his wedding to Princess Therese of Saxon-Hildburghausen?

A: Oktoberfest

INSECTS

1. Trees that are naturally resistant to damage by these insects include the turpentine tree, the teak tree, the white cypress and the sequoia.　**A: Termites**

2. Studies show that mosquitoes prefer to feed on people with this blood type.　**A: O**

3. What inch-long brown scarab beetle of the genus Phyllophaga appears in early summer?　**A: June Bug**

4. What aromatic yellow oil is used to repel insects?　**A: Citronella**

5. What domesticated insect prefers to eat white mulberry leaves?　**A: Silkworm**

6. What large biting insect is the primary vector of human sleeping sickness?　**A: Tsetse fly**

7. Most mosquitoes are crepuscular, which means they prefer to feed at this time of day.　**A: Dawn or dusk**

8. What fabric, named for the process by which it is made, is called the French word for caterpillar?　**A: Chenille**

9. What sugary, sticky liquid is secreted by aphids and other sap-sucking insects?　**A: Honeydew**

10. What insects help to reduce brush fire damage in African savannas by clearing away leaf and woody litter?　**A: Termites**

11. In the metamorphosis of an insect, what is the non-feeding stage between the larva and the adult?　**A: Pupa**

12. What notorious beetle lays its eggs in the buds of cotton plants, causing much damage?   **A: Boll weevil**

13. What predatory insect gets its name from the way it folds its fore-limbs?   **A: Praying mantis**

14. Some species of this insect stay burrowed in the ground 17 years before emerging as buzzing adults.   **A: Cicada (locust)**

15. To what "jointed leg" phylum do spiders belong?

A: Arthropod

16. These ants from the genus Solenopsis inject a toxic alkaloid venom into their bites.   **A: Fire ants**

17. What predatory insect, related to the dragonfly, has wings that fold together at rest?   **A: Damselfly**

18. The larvae of this American butterfly eat only milkweed.

A: Monarch

19. What insect's name has been Americanized from the Spanish word "cucaracha"?   **A: Cockroach**

20. These black and red insects feed almost exclusively on the seeds of Acer species.   **A: Box elder bugs**

21. These green insects, also called bush crickets or long-horned grasshoppers, are named for the sound of their mating call.

A: Katydids

22. Crickets "stridulate," or rub their _____ together, to attract a mate.   **A: Wings**

23. These insects have been decimated in North America by what

has been dubbed "colony collapse disorder."   **A: Honey bees**

24. This predatory wasp is the mascot of Georgia Tech.

A: Yellow jacket

25. The non-flying, slow moving Florida woods cockroach is also

known as a _____ bug.   **A: Palmetto**

INVENTORS AND INVENTIONS

1. What American engineer invented the first modern air conditioner in 1902?   **A: Willis Carrier**

2. What Scottish biologist discovered penicillin in 1928?

A: Alexander Fleming

3. This American engineer and industrialist invented the sleeping car in 1864.   **A: George Pullman**

4. This Swedish chemist and engineer held 350 patents, the most famous of which was dynamite.   **A: Alfred Nobel**

5. What American inventor received the first U.S. patent for a sewing machine using a lockstitch design?   **A: Elias Howe**

6. What unit of sound was named after the inventor of the telephone, Alexander Graham Bell?   **A: Decibel**

7. British engineer Hubert C. _____ invented the first powered vacuum cleaner.   **A: Booth**

8. What Italian physicist and astronomer invented the thermoscope, forerunner of the thermometer?   **A: Galileo**

9. What modeling compound was first manufactured as a wallpaper cleaner in the 1930s?   **A: Play-Doh**

10. What American industrialist designed the first passenger elevator with a safety device?   **A: Elisha Otis**

11. What Italian electrical engineer sent the first transatlantic wireless message in 1901?   **A: Guglielmo Marconi**

12. What Italian-born physicist helped to build Chicago Pile-1, the world's first nuclear reactor, in 1942?   **A: Enrico Fermi**

13. What American engineer and physicist built the first liquid fuel rocket which he launched on March 16, 1926?   **A: Robert Goddard**

14. What British engineer and inventor developed the process of purifying molten pig iron into steel with blasts of air?   **A: Henry Bessemer**

15. What ancient Greek mathematician is credited with designing the screw pump, compound pulleys and war machines to protect his city, Syracuse, from invasion?   **A: Archimedes**

16. This English potter developed a better formula for bone china and the durable china made from it is named after him.

A: Josiah Spode (Spodeware)

17. Many people have been credited with the invention of the electric telephone, but he was the first to be awarded a patent for it in 1876.   **A: Alexander Graham Bell**

18. What French chemist, known as the "father of microbiology," is best known for his technique of treating milk to stop bacterial contamination?   **A: Louis Pasteur**

19. Leo Baekeland developed this substance, the world's first synthetic plastic, in 1907 and it was named after him.   **A: Bakelite**

20. What German physicist invented the first mercury-in-glass thermometer in 1714?   **A: Gabriel Fahrenheit**

21. What French psychologist developed the first practical intelligence test around the turn of the 20th century to identify special needs students?   **A: Alfred Binet**

22. What medical engineer invented the artificial heart?

A: Robert Jarvik

23. What prolific American inventor held 1,093 patents and greatly impacted the world with his inventions?   **A: Thomas Edison**

24. What American theoretical physicist is known as the "father of the hydrogen bomb"?   **A: Edward Teller**

25. This Italian painter and inventor's journals included a large number of inventions, including musical instruments and fanciful flying machines.   **A: Leonardo da Vinci**

LITERATURE

1. What United States "Beat" generation poet wrote "Howl" in 1955?   **A: Allen Ginsberg**

2. What native Georgian wrote "Uncle Remus: His Songs and His Sayings"?   **A: Joel Chandler Harris**

3. What prolific English romance author wrote more than 700 books which sold more than 750 million copies?   **A: Barbara Cartland**

4. What English playwright wrote the 1941 black comedy "Blithe Spirit"?   **A: Noel Coward**

5. What Tennyson poem about the Crimean War begins "Half a league, half a league, half a league onward"?   **A: "The Charge of the Light Brigade"**

6. What American lexicographer first published "An American Dictionary of the English Language" in 1828?   **A: Noah Webster**

7. What American novelist won a Pulitzer Prize in fiction for "So Big" in 1924?   **A: Edna Ferber**

8. Harper Lee initially titled this 1960 Pulitzer-Prize winning novel "Atticus" but change it before publication.   **A: "To Kill A Mockingbird"**

9. What Louisa May Alcott book begins "Christmas won't be Christmas without any presents," grumbled Jo, lying on the rug"?   **A: "Little Women"**

10. What was the title of the only novel Sylvia Plath wrote?

A: "The Bell Jar"

11. What Italian Renaissance writer wrote "The Prince," a political treatise that advocated dispensing with the rules of morality if security required it?   **A: Niccolò Machiavelli**

12. What best-selling Sinclair Lewis novel was set in Gopher Prairie, a town modeled on his birthplace of Sauk Centre, Minnesota?

A: "Main Street"

13. What verse form was popularized by Edward Lear in the 19th century?   **A: Limerick**

14. What was the name of Winnie the Pooh's gloomy stuffed donkey friend?   **A: Eeyore**

15. What English Renaissance poet wrote "The Canterbury Tales" at the end of the 14th century?   **A: Geoffrey Chaucer**

16. What was the surname of John Steinbeck's family of Okie tenant farmers who set out for California to escape the Great Depression in "The Grapes of Wrath"?   **A: Joad**

17. What Welsh poet wrote an ode to his dying father in 1951 titled "Do not go gentle into that good night"?   **A: Dylan Thomas**

18. What 1719 book about the adventures of a shipwrecked man and his servant is considered by many to be the first novel written in English?   **A: "Robinson Crusoe"**

19. What American novelist wrote "The Hunt for Red October" and "Patriot Games"?   **A: Tom Clancy**

20. Charles Dickens' famous novel "A Tale of Two Cities" refers to what two cities?   **A: London and Paris**

21. What fictional Belgian detective appeared in 33 novels by Agatha Christie?   **A: Hercule Poirot**

22. What 1962 environmental science book by Rachel Carson warned us about the dangerous effects of pesticides on the environment?   **A: "Silent Spring"**

23. What American novelist stated that his best book-to-movie adaptations were "Stand by Me," "The Shawshank Redemption," and "The Mist"?   **A: Stephen King**

24. What 1940 novel about a collie by Eric Knight was made into the TV series "Lassie" and aired from 1954 to 1973?   **A: "Lassie Come-Home"**

25. What novel by Russian novelist Fyodor Dostoyevsky explored the moral dilemma of "Is murder acceptable in pursuit of a higher purpose?"?   **A: "Crime and Punishment"**

26. What American poet spent his entire life rewriting and revising his small book of poems "Leaves of Grass" until it eventually contained over 400 poems?   **A: Walt Whitman**

27. On what island did J. M. Barrie place the adventures of Peter Pan, Tinker Bell and the Darling family?   **A: Neverland**

28. The author of the poem "Trees" was killed by a sniper's bullet in World War I at the age of 31. Who was he?   **A: Joyce Kilmer**

29. What 1952 children's novel by E. B. White tells the story of a pig named Wilbur and his friendship with a spider?   **A: "Charlotte's Web"**

30. In poetry, what is the term for the repetition of the same or similar sounds at the beginning of words?   **A: Alliteration**

31. What reclusive American poet, often referred to as "The Belle of Amherst," wrote the poem "Because I could not stop for Death"?   **A: Emily Dickinson**

32. What 1865 novel by Mary Mapes Dodge provided a colorful snapshot of 19th century life in the Netherlands and introduced America to the Dutch sport of speed skating?   **A: "Hans Brinker, or The Silver Skates"**

33. What 19th century Danish spinner of fairy tales wrote "The Ugly Duckling" and "The Emperor's New Clothes"?   **A: Hans Christian Andersen**

34. What 1923 novel by Austrian Felix Salten about a male roe deer was banned in Nazi Germany in 1936 as "political allegory on the treatment of Jews in Europe"?   **A: "Bambi, a Life in the Woods"**

35. Name the Willa Cather novel from which came this first line: "I first heard of Ántonia on what seemed to me an interminable journey across the great midland plains of North America."
A: "My Antonia"

36. What author of "I Know Why the Caged Bird Sings" became mute from ages 8 to 13 after being sexually abused by her mother's boyfriend?   **A: Maya Angelou**

37. What 1843 novella by Charles Dickens begins "Marley was dead, to begin with. There is no doubt whatever about that."

A: "A Christmas Carol"

38. What epic poem by Dante Alighieri was an allegory of the soul's journey through Hell, Purgatory, and Heaven toward God?

A: "The Divine Comedy"

39. What fictional town where the Grinch stole a sleigh full of Christmas presents was said to be located inside a snowflake?

A: Whoville

40. Henry Wadsworth Longfellow's epic poem of 1855 featured an Ojibwe hero named what?   A: Hiawatha

41. Who is the protagonist of James Fenimore Cooper's five novels known collectively as "The Leatherstocking Tales"?   A: Natty Bumppo

42. What is the term for a writing style or form used to convey the opposite of their literal meaning?   A: Irony

43. The diary kept by this English Admiralty official and MP is one of the best eyewitness accounts of the events of the English Restoration period.   A: Samuel Pepys

44. Grace Metalious was 30 when she began work on this manuscript about the dark secrets of a town in New England.

A: "Peyton Place"

45. What American novelist and social critic wrote "The Fire Next Time," "Notes of a Native Son," and "Go, Tell It on the Mountain"?   A: James Baldwin

46. The English poet Thomas Gray wrote, "The paths of glory lead but to the grave, and far from the _____ crowd's ignoble strife, their sober wishes never learned to stray."   **A: Madding**

47. U.S. humorist James Thurber wrote "The Secret Life of _____ _____."   **A: Walter Mitty**

48. What novel by Carson McCullers begins, "In the town there were two mutes, and they were always together"?   **A: "The Heart is a Lonely Hunter"**

49. What is the best-known work of Massachusetts poet William Cullent Bryant?   **A: "Thanatopsis"**

50. What book by Polish-born author Joseph Conrad was the basis of Coppola's "Apocalypse Now"?   **A: "Heart of Darkness"**

MAGAZINES AND NEWSPAPERS

1. One of the most famous covers of this Condé Nast publication was an August 1991 Annie Leibovitz cover of a nude and pregnant Demi Moore.   **A: Vanity Fair**

2. What Midwestern newspaper ran the famous 1948 "Dewey Defeats Truman" headline?   **A: Chicago Tribune**

3. Humorist Dave Barry writes a column for this McClatchy Company newspaper.   **A: Miami Herald**

4. Modern Maturity was the former name of this senior citizen interest group's publication.   **A: AARP**

5. In 1903, this women's magazine became the first American magazine to reach one million subscribers.   **A: Ladies' Home Journal**

6. Reporters Bob Woodward and Carl Bernstein first broke the Watergate scandal in this newspaper.   **A: Washington Post**

7. This newspaper is not only the largest daily newspaper in Connecticut, it's the oldest continuously published newspaper in the U.S.   **A: Hartford Courant**

8. Twenty-five million now read this weekly news magazine founded by Briton Hadden and Henry Luce in 1923.   **A: Time magazine**

9. This magazine founded by Dr. Norman Vincent Peale and his wife Ruth in 1945 contains testimonies about how faith in God helped in personal challenges.   **A: Guideposts**

10. What American daily newspaper's motto is "All the News That's Fit to Print"? **A: The New York Times**

11. This magazine which presents scientific information is the oldest continuously published monthly magazine in the United States. **A: Scientific American**

12. What newspaper magnate's life was the inspiration for the lead character in the movie "Citizen Kane"? **A: William Randolph Hearst**

13. What former talk show host writes a regular column showcasing his car collection and giving automotive advice in "Popular Mechanics"? **A: Jay Leno**

14. Founded by a former secretary of agriculture, this magazine was originally called Fruit, Gardener and Home. **A: Better Homes and Gardens**

15. What Condé Nast magazine, whose name means "style" in French, targeted the New York aristocracy from its inception in 1892? **A: Vogue**

16. This daily American newspaper is nicknamed "The Gray Lady." **A: New York Times**

17. What magazine, named after a Thackeray novel, revealed the identity of the Watergate scandal's "Deep Throat" in May of 2005? **A: Vanity Fair**

18. What woman became chief editor of Cosmopolitan in 1965 and re-invented it as a magazine for single career women? **A: Helen Gurley Brown**

19. What Michigan newspaper is the largest city newspaper owned by Gannett, which also publishes national newspaper USA Today?

A: **Detroit Free Press**

20. What men's magazine discontinued its annual "Dubious Achievement Awards" in 2008?   A: **Esquire**

21. What magazine's annual swimsuit issue is credited with making the bikini, invented in 1946, a legitimate piece of apparel?

A: **Sports Illustrated**

22. What compact consumer magazine has a global circulation of 10.5 million, making it the largest paid circulation magazine in the world?   A: **Reader's Digest**

23. What humor magazine featured a John Hughes' short story titled "Vacation '58," which inspired a whole series of comedy films featuring the Griswold family?   A: **National Lampoon**

24. What digest-sized magazine's inaugural cover in April of 1953 featured a photograph of Lucille Ball's newborn son Desi Arnaz Jr.?   A: **TV Guide**

25. What Boston newspaper's chief print rival is the Boston Herald?   A: **The Boston Globe**

MATHEMATICS

1. What is the name of the branch of mathematics which deals with the collection and analysis of numerical data?   **A: Statistics**

2. What is the only even prime number?   **A: 2**

3. What is the mathematical unit of measurement of an angle or an arc?   **A: Degree**

4. The Roman numeral "M" is equal to this number.   **A: 1000**

5. What is the term for the number written below the line in a fraction?   **A: Denominator**

6. What is the square root of 900?   **A: 30**

7. A one followed by 12 zeroes is what number?   **A: Trillion**

8. What number is 10 to the 100th power?   **A: Googol**

9. What is the mathematical term for a perfectly round object with all points on its surface the same distance from the center?

A: Sphere

10. What number has a cube root of 4 and a square root of 8?

A: 64

11. What is the mathematical term for twice the radius of a circle times pi?   **A: Circumference**

12. Two lines that intersect to form right angles are what kind of lines?   **A: Perpendicular**

13. How many degrees is a straight angle?   **A: 180**

14. What geometrical figure is four-sided with two of its sides parallel?   **A: Trapezoid**

15. What type of triangle has two equal sides?   **A: Isosceles**

16. What is the mathematical reciprocal of 5?   **A: 1/5**

17. What is the mathematical term for a line segment that joins the center of a circle with any point on its circumference?   **A: Radius**

18. What mathematical prefix is used to denote one billionth of something?   **A: Nano**

19. What type of triangle has three unequal sides?   **A: Scalene**

20. What is the term for two lines in the same plane that never intersect?   **A: Parallel lines**

21. What is the mathematical term for a nine-sided figure?

A: Nonagon

22. What branch of mathematics derives its name from that fact that it formerly dealt only with the collection and analysis of facts about a state?   **A: Statistics**

23. What is the term for the point of a number series which divides it so that half the quantities are on one side and half on the other?

A: Median

24. What is the name given to the longest side of a right-angled triangle?   **A: Hypotenuse**

25. What is the term for the geometrical study of two-dimensional figures?   **A: Plane geometry**

MEDICINE

1. What is the medical term for a subnormal body temperature?   **A: Hypothermia**

2. What is the more common term for "eructation"?   **A: Belching**

3. What mild infectious disease, transmitted to humans by milking infected cows, offers immunity to smallpox?   **A: Cowpox**

4. What type of cancer has the highest mortality rate for cancer in the United States?   **A: Lung**

5. What is the term for the complete set of an organism's genetic material?   **A: Genome**

6. How long after getting a tattoo in states that don't regulate tattoo facilities does the American Red Cross require one to wait to donate blood?   **A: One year**

7. What pandemic that began in January of 1918 killed 50 to 100 million people world-wide?   **A: Spanish flu**

8. What devastating pandemic of the 1400s was caused by the Yersinia pestis bacterium?   **A: Black Death**

9. What illness, spread through saliva, is caused by the Epstein-Barr virus?   **A: Mononucleosis**

10. What scale is used to evaluate the health of newborn babies immediately after birth?   **A: Apgar score**

11. What eating disorder is characterized by bouts of over-eating followed by purging?   **A: Bulimia**

12. What is the medical term for a congenital defect in which a longitudinal fissure exists in the roof of the mouth?   **A: Cleft palate**

13. What severe type of anemia is caused by the stomach's failure to absorb vitamin B12?   **A: Pernicious anemia**

14. What type of birth is characterized by an infant presenting in the birth canal feet or buttocks first?   **A: Breech**

15. What occupational lung disease is caused by inhalation of crystalline silica dust by miners, stonecutters and sandblasters?   **A: Silicosis**

16. What is the medical term for the inflammation of a vein?   **A: Phlebitis**

17. What endemic disease marked by copious diarrhea is spread mostly through contaminated drinking water and unsanitary conditions?   **A: Cholera**

18. What heart valve controls blood flow between the left atrium and left ventricle?   **A: Mitral valve**

19. What gland is enlarged when one is diagnosed with a goiter?   **A: Thyroid**

20. What is the more common term for "Creutzfeldt-Jakob disease"?   **A: Mad cow disease**

21. What substance, obtained from the foxglove plant, is used to treat heart failure?   **A: Digitalis**

22. What specific types of circulatory system cells carry oxygen throughout the body?   **A: Red blood cells**

23. What disease characterized by stabbing pain is caused by a reactivation of the varicella (chickenpox) virus?   A: **Shingles**

24. What is the medical term for diseases that can be spread from animals to humans under natural conditions?   A: **Zoonoses**

25. What highly contagious respiratory tract disease is formally known as pertussis?   A: **Whooping cough**

26. What is the medical term for light-headedness or fainting caused by insufficient blood supply to the brain?   A: **Syncope**

27. What is the proper medical term for the nostrils?   A: **Nares**

28. What is the medical term for an abnormally slow pulse?

A: **Bradycardia**

29. What insignia is a traditional symbol of the medical profession?   A: **Caduceus**

30. What long gland behind the stomach manufactures insulin and digestive enzymes?   A: **Pancreas**

31. What does a sphygmomanometer measure?   A: **Blood pressure**

32. What type of physician specializes in disorders of the anus and rectum? A: **Proctologist**

33. What type of physician identifies diseases by studying cells and tissues under a microscope?   A: **Pathologist**

34. What is the medical term for shortness of breath? A: **Dyspnea**

35. What flexible band of fibrous tissue connects the bones and binds the joints together?   A: **Ligament**

36. What is the medical term for all chemical substances produced by the endocrine glands?   **A: Hormones**

37. What flap of cartilage located at the root of the tongue prevents food from entering the windpipe during swallowing?

A: Epiglottis

38. What disease is the leading cause of adult blindness in the U.S.?   **A: Diabetes**

39. What is the proper medical term for the breastbone?

A: Sternum

40. What is the proper medical term for inflammation of the skin?   **A: Dermatitis**

41. "Otitis" is the general term for inflammation of what? **A: Ear**

42. "Singletus" is the medical term for what common ailment?

A: Hiccup

43. Who pioneered antiseptic surgery in England in 1867?

A: Joseph Lister

44. The term "hepatic" means "of or relating to" what organ?

A: Liver

45. What is the term for an insect or other organism that carries disease-causing micro-organisms from one host to another?

A: Vector

46. If you have "gingivitis," you have inflammation of what?

A: Gums

47. "Acetylsalicylic acid" is better known as what common medication?   **A: Aspirin**

48. What type of cancer is the most common cancer in males in 84 countries, occurring more commonly in the developed world?

A: Prostate cancer

49. What is the medical term for the chambers of the heart which contract to pump blood into arteries?   A: Ventricles

50. What color flag is flown by a ship to warn of disease on board?   A: Yellow

MONEY AND FINANCE

1. What was the former monetary unit of modern Greece?

A: **Drachma**

2. What type of bond is issued by a state, city or local government to raise capital?　　A: **Municipal bond**

3. What is the proper term for an unregistered negotiable bond on which interest and principal are payable to the holder?

A: **Bearer bond**

4. What is the aggregate term for the producers and manufacturers of agricultural goods and services, including wholesalers and retailers?　　A: **Agribusiness**

5. What is the term for investment companies who invest largely in companies developing new ideas or products?　　A: **Venture capital**

6. What type of market is characterized by a steady upward trend in the prices of corporate stocks?　　A: **Bull market**

7. Who served as Chairman of the Federal Reserve Board from 1987 to 2006?　　A: **Alan Greenspan**

8. What is the term for a monetary system in which the basic unit of currency is equal to a fixed quantity of gold?　　A: **Gold standard**

9. What currency unit was introduced into world physical circulation on January 1, 2002 by member states of the European Union?　　A: **Euro**

10. What federal agency regulates the exchange of securities and enforces federal securities laws to protect investors?   **A: U.S. Securities and Exchange Commission (SEC)**

11. What is the term for any form of money recognized by a government as valid for meeting debts and obligations?   **A: Legal tender**

12. What is the term for the practice of lending money and charging interest at an exorbitant rate which unfairly enriches the lender?   **A: Usury**

13. What is the term for the speculative practice of buying and selling securities on the same trading day?   **A: Day trading**

14. What is the term for a business professional who calculates financial risk?   **A: Actuary**

15. What is the main currency unit in nine Middle Eastern countries, including Iraq, Kuwait and Libya?   **A: Dinar**

16. What is the term for the payment made from a company's profits to its holders of common and preferred stocks?

A: Dividend

17. What type of tax increases as the amount of one's income increases?   **A: Progressive**

18. What economic theory is the idea that financial benefits accorded to big business will benefit smaller members by improving the economy as a whole?   **A: Trickle-down**

19. What is the smallest denomination of coin in Australia and Canada?   **A: 5 cent piece**

20. What government spending and public works program was implemented by President Franklin D. Roosevelt in response to the Great Depression?   **A: New Deal**

21. What is the real estate term for the dollar difference between what a property could be sold for and what is owed against it?   **A: Equity**

22. What American journalist founded the Wall Street Journal as well as an index of market statistics?   **A: Charles Henry Dow**

23. What is the proper term for assets that can be rapidly converted into money?   **A: Liquid**

24. What type of debt securities are issued by companies with higher than normal credit risk but offer a higher yield to compensate?   **A: Junk bonds**

25. What is the term for the exchange of goods or services without the use of money?   **A: Barter**

MOVIES

1. Who won a Best Supporting Actress Oscar for her role in the 1982 movie "Tootsie"? **A: Jessica Lange**

2. What 2014 film starred Benedict Cumberbatch as mathematician Alan Turing who cracked the Enigma code during World War II?

A: "The Imitation Game"

3. What precocious American child movie star always had exactly 56 curls in her hair? **A: Shirley Temple**

4. Madonna played centerfielder Mae Morabito in what 1992 film? **A: "A League of Their Own"**

5. What star of the silent romantic drama "The Sheikh" was known as the cinema screen's first great lover? **A: Rudolf Valentino**

6. What 2014 movie starring James Franco and Seth Rogen on a mission to assassinate dictator Kim Jong-un was called "the movie of terrorism" by North Korea? **A: "The Interview"**

7. Bette Midler's first platinum-selling album was the soundtrack for what 1979 drama about a self-destructive rock star? **A: "The Rose"**

8. Who won the 1938 Oscar for "Best Actress" for her role in "Jezebel"? **A: Bette Davis**

9. What 2012 Steven Soderbergh film featured Channing Tatum and Matthew McConaughey as male strippers? **A: "Magic Mike"**

10. The 1987 comedy-fantasy film "Witches of Eastwick" starred Cher, Susan Sarandon and what other actress? **A: Michelle Pfeiffer**

11. What 2013 film starring Leonardo DiCaprio was based on the true story of a wealthy stockbroker falling to crime and corruption? **A: "The Wolf of Wall Street"**

12. What group of brothers recorded the best-selling soundtrack to the 1977 film "Saturday Night Fever"? **A: Bee Gees**

13. Faye Dunaway portrayed Joan Crawford in this 1981 biographical drama. **A: "Mommie Dearest"**

14. Julianne Moore won a "Best Actress" Oscar for her perform-ance as a linguistics professor struggling with Alzheimer's Disease in this 2014 film. **A: "Still Alice"**

15. Clint Eastwood said in this 1971 action film, "You've got to ask yourself one question: 'Do I feel lucky?' Well, do ya punk?"

A: "Dirty Harry"

16. Who played Warrant Officer Ripley in the 1986 movie "Aliens"?

A: Sigourney Weaver

17. Shailene Woodley starred in this 2014 film about two cancer victims who meet at a cancer support group and fall in love.

A: "The Fault in Our Stars"

18. The word "supercalifragilisticexpialidocious" originated in what 1964 musical? **A: "Mary Poppins"**

19. Who won a "Best Actress" Oscar in 1990 for her role in the psychological thriller "Misery"? **A: Kathy Bates**

20. What was the name of the all-girl Barden University a cappella singing group in the 2012 musical comedy "Pitch Perfect"?

A: The (Barden) Bellas

21. Who was a co-star and director of the 1987 black comedy "Throw Momma From The Train"?   **A: Danny Devito**

22. Who won an Oscar for his portrayal of the character "Popeye Doyle" in the 1971 thriller "The French Connection"?   **A: Gene Hackman**

23. What 2013 Oscar-winning film was the memoir of the life of Solomon Northup, a free black man who was abducted and sold into slavery?   **A: "12 Years a Slave"**

24. What 1991 thriller featured the closing line "I do wish we could talk longer, but I'm having an old friend for dinner"?   **A: "Silence of the Lambs"**

25. What actress's mother is best-known for her performance in the 1988 film "Working Girl" and her grandmother for her lead role in Alfred Hitchcock's 1963 horror film "The Birds"?   **A: Dakota Johnson**

26. Owen Wilson and Vince Vaughn starred in this 2005 film about a pair of womanizers who sneak into weddings to meet women.

A: "Wedding Crashers"

27. What star of "Dirty Dancing" died in 2009 of pancreatic cancer?   **A: Patrick Swayze**

28. Elizabeth Taylor received a record-setting $7 million in what 1963 extravaganza that almost bankrupted 20th Century Fox? A: **"Cleopatra"**

29. What 2008 thriller starred Liam Neeson as a retired CIA agent using his considerable skills across Europe to rescue his kidnapped daughter? **A: "Taken"**

30. Who played Freddy Krueger in the 1984 horror film "A Nightmare on Elm Street"? **A: Robert Englund**

31. What 1967 Mike Nichols film opened with the song, "The Sounds of Silence"? **A: "The Graduate"**

32. What Oscar-winning 2007 Joel and Ethan Coen film starring Tommy Lee Jones and Javier Bardem took its name from W. B. Yeats poem "Sailing to Byzantium"? **A: "No Country for Old Men"**

33. What "Dick Tracy" star is the brother of actress Shirley MacLaine? **A: Warren Beatty**

34. What romantic comedy starring Claudette Colbert and Clark Gable won all five major academy awards in 1934? **A: "It Happened One Night"**

35. What 2006 Martin Scorsese crime drama about the tangled relationship between the Irish mob and the Massachusetts State Police won the "Best Picture" Oscar? **A: "The Departed"**

36. What star of "Beetlejuice," "Edward Scissorhands," and "Girl, Interrupted" was named after the Minnesota city in which she was born? **A: Winona Ryder**

37. What 1985 drama was notable for the dancing of Gregory Hines and Mikhail Baryshnikov as well as Lionel Richie's Oscar-winning song "Say You, Say Me"?   **A: "White Nights"**

38. What 2005 computer-animated film tells the story of four Central Park Zoo animals who get shipwrecked on an African island?   **A: "Madagascar"**

39. What actor was killed filming a battle scene in 1982's "Twilight Zone: The Movie" when a stunt helicopter crashed on him?

A: Vic Morrow

40. What cowboy star of 282 silent movies became Hollywood's first Western megastar?   **A: Tom Mix**

41. What 2005 movie starring Jake Gyllenhaal and Heath Ledger was the story of a forbidden relationship between two cow-boys?   **A: "Brokeback Mountain"**

42. Who was the director of the 1987 war film "Full Metal Jacket"?   **A: Stanley Kubrick**

43. What star of "Singing in the Rain" published her tell-all autobiography "Unsinkable" in 2013?   **A: Debbie Reynolds**

44. What 2006 fashion magazine industry film starring Meryl Streep was widely believed to have been inspired by "Vogue" editor Anna Wintour?   **A: "The Devil Wears Prada"**

45. What 1976 Western film was John Wayne's final film role?

A: "The Shootist"

46. What instrumental bluegrass composition was made famous by the 1972 film "Deliverance"?   **A: "Dueling Banjos"**

47. Who starred in the 2006 film "Night at the Museum" as a newly-hired night security guard who discovered that the exhibits come to life and wreak havoc at night?   **A: Ben Stiller**

48. What major film studio is represented by a snowcapped mountain circled by stars?   **A: Paramount**

49. What actress's famous "red swimsuit" poster was a best seller of its time?   **A: Farrah Fawcett**

50. What actor's last film before dying of an accidental overdose of prescription drugs in 2008 was "The Imaginarium of Doctor Par-nassus"?   **A: Heath Ledger**

MUSIC

1. What country singer's 1979 autobiography "Stand By Your Man" was a New York Times best-seller?   **A: Tammy Wynette**

2. What country group introduced their signature song "Elvira" in 1981?   **A: Oak Ridge Boys**

3. What is the proper term for a short ceremonial flourish typically played by trumpets and other brass to introduce something or someone important?   **A: Fanfare**

4. This danceable style of American music by big bands was the dominant form of popular music from 1935 to 1946.   **A: Swing**

5. What instrument invented by German inventor Maelzel in 1816 is used to indicate the exact tempo of a musical composition?

A: Metronome

6. What song by Willie Nelson which won the Grammy for "Best County Song" in 1981 was the theme for Nelson's 1980 movie "Honeysuckle Rose"?   **A: "On the Road Again"**

7. What one word is missing from the following song titles? "_____ Day Women #12 & 35," "Here Comes That _____ Day Feelin' Again," and "_____ Night in Georgia."   **A: Rainy**

8. What word or phrase is missing from the following song titles? "Sidewalks of _____," "The Only Living Boy in _____," and "_____ State of Mind."   **A: New York**

9. What large brass instrument designed to be played in marching bands was named after the March King?   **A: Sousaphone**

96

10. What keyboard instrument widely used in Renaissance music was a precursor of the piano?   **A: Harpsichord**

11. Before 1770, this double reed woodwind instrument was called a hautbois (high woodwind).   **A: Oboe**

12. What stringed instrument's name literally means "sweet song"?   **A: Dulcimer**

13. What percussion instruments are also known as "clackers" in the United States?   **A: Castanets**

14. What Stephen Foster song begins "Way down upon the Swanee River, far far away . . ."?   **A: "The Old Folks at Home"**

15. Accompanied by his brass ensemble, this musician had hits with "The Lonely Bull," "Whipped Cream," and "A Taste of Honey" in the 1960s.   **A: Herb Alpert**

16. Which country artist wrote "Crazy," "Hello Walls" and "Pretty Paper"?   **A: Willie Nelson**

17. This 1959 album was not only Miles Davis' best-selling album, but it may be the best-selling jazz record of all time.   **A: "Kind of Blue"**

18. What country artist had a series of hits in the 1960s and 1970s that included "Gentle On My Mind" and "By the Time I Get to Phoenix"?   **A: Glen Campbell**

19. What term that literally means "in the manner of the chapel" refers to music sung without instrumental accompaniment?
A: A cappella

20. What musical accidental lowers a note by a half step?   **A: Flat**

21. Commonly used by groups such as the Beach Boys, this type of singing is done by a male voice in a register above its usual range.   **A: Falsetto**

22. What Italian operatic tenor, born in 1873, became one of the first examples of a global media celebrity because of his recordings?   **A: Enrico Caruso**

23. What style of music popular in southern Louisiana is played by a small group featuring a guitar, an accordion and a washboard?

A: Zydeco

24. What song from the film "The Big Broadcast of 1938" became Bob Hope's signature tune?   **A: "Thanks for the Memories"**

25. What Grammy-winning choir holds a yearly Christmas concert in Salt Lake City?   **A: Mormon Tabernacle Choir**

26. What Edward Elgar march is played as the processional tune at countless high school and college graduation ceremonies in the United States?   **A: "Pomp and Circumstance" or "Land of Hope and Glory"**

27. What signature song of Tony Bennet is one of the official anthems for a major California city?   **A: "I Left My Heart in San Francisco"**

28. What traditional southwestern Virginia folk group was elected to the Country Music Hall of Fame in 1970 and given the nickname "The First Family of Country Music"?   **A: The Carter Family**

29. On December 31, 1956, this big band leader had his first New Year's TV special on CBS with a live segment from Times Square.

A: Guy Lombardo

30. What female artist won the "Album of the Year" Grammy in 1964 with her album "People"?   **A: Barbra Streisand**

31. What popular swing/boogie-woogie group had World War II hits with "(I'll Be With You) In Apple Blossom Time" and "Don't Sit Under the Apple Tree"?   **A: The Andrews Sisters**

32. What trumpet virtuoso – along with Charlie Parker – helped to develop bebop and modern jazz in the 1940s?   **A: Dizzy Gillespie**

33. Who was the first African-American woman to sing with the Metropolitan Opera of New York City?   **A: Marian Anderson**

34. Louis Armstrong introduced this singing of meaningless syllables in place of words.   **A: Scat singing**

35. What Caribbean-American had the first million-selling album by a solo artist with his breakthrough album "Calypso" in 1956?

A: Harry Belafonte

36. What 1955 song by Bill Haley became the first rock and roll song to top Billboard magazine's main sales and air play charts?

A: "Rock Around the Clock"

37. What #1 hit by The Shirelles in 1960 was written by Gerry Goffin and Carole King?   **A: "Will You Love Me Tomorrow?"**

38. What 1965 song by the Righteous Brothers is listed by Broadcast Music Incorporated as the song with the most American

airplay in the 20th century?   **A: "You've Lost that Lovin' Feelin'"**

39. The drum solo for this 1966 surf music hit by The Surfaris was one of the best-remembered instrumental tunes of the 60s.

A: "Wipe Out"

40. What "British Invasion" group of the 1960s became the biggest selling rock band of all time?   **A: the Beatles**

41. This 1971 Led Zeppelin hit featuring a guitar solo by Jimmy Page is often considered one of the greatest rock songs of all time.

A: "Stairway to Heaven"

42. By 1963 this singer/songwriter of folk rock had gone mainstream with his hits, including "Blowin' in the Wind." **A: Bob Dylan**

43. This singer's 1966 hit album "Sunshine Superman" was one of the first psychedelic pop records.   **A: Donovan**

44. What soft rock group's album "Rumours" was the best-selling album of the 1970s?   **A: Fleetwood Mac**

45. Whose "heartland rock" album "Born in the USA," released in 1984, topped the charts all over the world?   **A: Bruce Springsteen**

46. "Smells Like Teen Spirit" was the lead single on this grunge group's 1991 album "Nevermind."   **A: Nirvana**

47. What punk rock group's 1994 album "Dookie" spawned the hit singles "Longview," "When I Come Around," "Basket Case," "Welcome to Paradise" and "She"?   **A: Green Day**

48. What 1969 music festival was billed, "An Aquarian Exposition: 3

Days of Peace & Music"?   **A: Woodstock**

49. What music genre has four elements: rap music, DJing, b-boying and graffiti art?   **A: Hip hop**

50. What founding father of funk music is known as "The Godfather of Soul"?   **A: James Brown**

MUSICALS AND BROADWAY

1. What Tony Award-winning musical was adapted from the Thornton Wilder play "The Matchmaker"?   **A: "Hello, Dolly!"**

2. What two Victorian-era men collaborated on the comic operas "H.M.S. Pinafore," "The Pirates of Penzance" and "The Mikado"?   **A: Gilbert and Sullivan**

3. What 1927 musical by Jerome Kern and Oscar Hammerstein II about interracial love was based on a best-selling Edna Ferber novel?   **A: "Showboat"**

4. What 1943 Rodgers and Hammerstein musical tells the story of cowboy Curly McLain and his romance with farm girl Laurey Williams in 1906 Oklahoma Territory?   **A: "Oklahoma"**

5. Leonard Bernstein wrote "I Feel Pretty" and "Maria" for this 1957 Broadway production.   **A: "West Side Story"**

6. What 1968 rock musical featured songs like "Aquarius," "Easy to Be Hard" and "Good Morning Starshine"?   **A: "Hair"**

7. What 1975 Marvin Hamlisch musical about auditioning Broadway dancers featured the number "What I Did for Love"?
A: "A Chorus Line"

8. What 2003 Broadway musical told an "alternative" story about the witches from "The Wizard of Oz"?   **A: "Wicked"**

9. What type of multi-act theatrical production combines music, dance and sketches?   **A: Revue**

10. What type of theater production features actors performing spontaneously?   A: **Improv/Improvisational**

11. What Shakespearean character begins his famous soliloquy with "To be or not to be: That is the question"?   A: **Hamlet**

12. What Henrik Ibsen play features the protagonist Nora Helmer, who leaves her husband to discover herself?   A: **"A Doll's House"**

13. What Thornton Wilder play set in Grover's Corners in 1938 "breaks the fourth wall" and allows the narrator to address the audience directly?   A: **"Our Town"**

14. What playwright's epitaph is: "Good friend, for Jesus' sake forbear / To dig the dust enclosed here / Blessed be the man that spares these stones / And cursed be he that moves my bones"?
A: **William Shakespeare**

15. What playwright, author of "Brighton Beach Memoirs," has received more combined Oscar and Tony nominations than any other writer?   A: **Neil Simon**

16. What musical inspired by Cervantes' "Don Quixote" features the song "The Impossible Dream"?   A: **"Man of La Mancha"**

17. Meredith Wilson was inspired by his boyhood home in Mason City, Iowa to write this musical featuring the song "Till There Was You."   A: **"The Music Man"**

18. Marlon Brando played the part of Stanley Kowalski in this Tennessee Williams play which opened on Broadway in 1947.
A: **"A Streetcar Named Desire"**

19. What 1945 Rodgers and Hammerstein musical featured the well-known songs "June is Bustin' Out All Over" and "You'll Never Walk Alone"?   **A: "Carousel"**

20. What 1943 Broadway production opened with the number "Oh, What a Beautiful Mornin'"?   **A: "Oklahoma"**

21. What 1951 Lerner and Loewe musical featured the songs "Wand'rin' Star," "I Talk to the Trees" and "They Call the Wind Maria"?   **A: "Paint Your Wagon"**

22. What Nobel-winning Irish playwright's socialist views were evident in his plays "Pygmalion" and "Major Barbara"?

A: George Bernard Shaw

23. What American dramatist wrote "Come Back, Little Sheba," "Bus Stop," and "Picnic"?   **A: William Inge**

24. What award is given for excellence in an off-Broadway performance?   **A: Obie**

25. What Nobel-winning American dramatist wrote "Mourning Becomes Electra," "Anna Christie," and "The Iceman Cometh"?

A: Eugene O'Neill

MYTHOLOGY

1. It is a Scandinavian folk belief that lightning frightens away these ugly, hostile beings, some of who might live under a bridge?

A: Trolls

2. This race of dwarves are featured in Richard Wagner's four-opera cycle about a ring made of Rheingold.   **A: "Nibelung"**

3. On what legendary island was King Arthur's sword Excalibur forged?   **A: Avalon**

4. The name of an opiate drug is derived from the name of this ancient Greek god of dreams.   **A: Morpheus**

5. What mythical creature with the head of a woman and the body of a lion will kill and eat you if you cannot answer her riddle?

A: The sphinx

6. These handmaidens of Odin accompanied slain warriors from the battlefield to Valhalla.   **A: Valkyries**

7. What Egyptian god of the afterlife had the head of an African wolf?   **A: Anubis**

8. What major Roman god is often depicted as a winged messenger?   **A: Mercury**

9. What Greek goddess of the moon drives her moon chariot across the heavens?   **A: Selene**

10. The Romans held festivals of supposed drunkenness and debauchery in honor of this Greco-Roman god of wine. **A: Bacchus**

11. What beautiful Greek youth/god died in Aphrodite's arms after being wounded by a wild boar?   **A: Adonis**

12. What month of the year, the beginning of both farming and warfare, is named after the Roman god of war?   **A: March (Mars)**

13. Who was the lover of Guinevere, wife of King Arthur?

A: Lancelot

14. In ancient Greece, a coin was sometimes placed in the mouth of a deceased person to pay this ferryman of Hades to carry him/her across the River Styx.   **A: Charon**

15. For opposing Zeus in battle, this defeated Titan was condemned to support the vault of the heavens upon his shoulders.   **A: Atlas**

16. A type of syncopated West Indian music is named after this mythological Greek sea nymph who detained Odysseus for seven years.   **A: Calypso**

17. What mythological Greek king was condemned to roll a heavy stone up a hill in Hades only to have it roll down again as it nears the top?   **A: Sisyphus**

18. Who was the Greek mythological daughter of Tantalus who, while crying for her slain children, is turned into a weeping stone?   **A: Niobe**

19. What day of the week is named after the Norse god of fertility, sun and rain?   **A: Friday (Frey)**

20. Who was the god of the north wind in Greek mythology?

A: Boreas

21. Which of the Seven Wonders of the Ancient World was a statue of Helios, the Greek god of the sun?   **A: Colossus of Rhodes**

22. Who was the Roman god of fire and metalworking?   **A: Vulcan**

23. Norse heroes slain in battle were received into this majestic hall of Odin in Asgard.   **A: Valhalla**

24. Who was the ancient Egyptian goddess of nature and magic?

A: Isis

25. "Shrek" was one of these large, hideous monsters from mythology and folklore but he didn't eat human beings.   **A: Ogre**

POLITICS AND GOVERNMENT

1. What Montana Republican was the first woman to be elected to Congress (1916)?   **A: Jeanette Rankin**

2. What campaign aide was the nemesis of presidential candidate Gary Hart in 1987?   **A: Donna Rice**

3. The four states which officially refer to themselves as "The Commonwealth" are Massachusetts, Virginia, Kentucky and this one.   **A: Pennsylvania**

4. What is the term for a research group organized by a government or advocacy group for solving complex problems?   **A: Think tank**

5. What trade agreement approved by Congress in 1993 eliminated trade barriers between the U. S., Canada, and Mexico?   **A: NAFTA (North American Free Trade Agreement)**

6. What was the policy of giving U. S. economic aid to the nations of Europe after World War II to help them rebuild their war-torn economies?   **A: Marshall Plan (European Recovery Program)**

7. A "plutocracy" is government by a small minority of this class of citizens.   **A: Wealthy**

8. What Secretary of State erroneously declared "I am in control here" moments after President Reagan was shot in March of 1981?   **A: Alexander Haig**

9. What is the term for the British civil service?   **A: Whitehall**

10. What is the term for the working class in socialist philo-sophy?   **A: Proletariat**

11. A pleasure trip made by a public official at public expense is called this.   **A: Junket**

12. A public declaration of political principles, such as a certain famous one written by Karl Marx, is called this.   **A: Manifesto**

13. What is the term for a president's indirect veto of a bill by keeping the bill unsigned until the legislature adjourns?

A: Pocket veto

14. What does the "A" stand for in the international acronym N.A.T.O.?   **A: Atlantic (North Atlantic Treaty Organization)**

15. What body formally chooses the president of the United States?   **A: Electoral college**

16. The approval of what fraction of each house of Congress and of the states is required to amend the United States Constitution?

A: Two-thirds

17. What 1980s political scandal featured FBI agents posing as Arab businessmen seeking political favors from U.S. congressmen?

A: Abscam

18. What was the official term for the Clinton policy that attempted to end discrimination against homosexuals in the U. S. military?

A: Don't Ask, Don't Tell

19. What program established by President John F. Kennedy in 1961 sought to assist developing countries by sending American volunteers to teach and to provide technical assistance?

A: Peace Corps

20. What is the term for a vote taken directly by the general public to decide an important legislative or policy issue (rather than having the issue decided by a representative assembly or other legislative agency)?   **A: Referendum**

21. Which cabinet department commands the U.S. Coast Guard during peacetime?   **A: Department of Homeland Security**

22. What Speaker of the House helped to co-write the 1994 Republican policy document "Contract With America"?   **A: Newt Gingrich**

23. What Minnesota Democrat was the first major presidential contender to protest U. S. involvement in Vietnam (1968)?

A: Eugene McCarthy

24. What controversial policy seeks to redress past discrimination by ensuring equal opportunity, as in education and employment?

A: Affirmative action

25. What specific provision of the U.S. Constitution gives Congress the authority to regulate trade with foreign nations and among the states?   **A: Commerce clause**

QUOTATIONS

1. What famous defense attorney said, "Not only did we play the race card, we dealt it from the bottom of the deck."   **A: Robert Shapiro**

2. What prolific Maine novelist declared, "I am the literary equivalent of a Big Mac and fries"?   **A: Stephen King**

3. What famed American sportscaster said, "What does a mama bear on the pill have in common with the World Series? No Cubs."?   **A: Harry Caray**

4. What British prime minister, asking the House of Commons to declare its confidence in his government, famously declared, "I have nothing to offer but blood, toil, tears, and sweat"?   **A: Winston Churchill**

5. What famous American newsman ended his broadcasts with, "And that's the way it is . . ."?   **A: Walter Cronkite**

6. What famous movie character said, "Stupid is as stupid does"?   **A: Forrest Gump**

7. What French military and political leader said, "An army marches on its stomach"?   **A: Napoleon Bonaparte**

8. What "wild and crazy guy" had the trademark phrase "Well excuuuuuuuuuuuuuuuuuse ME!"?   **A: Steve Martin**

9. Her character Ernestine said, "One ringy-dingy. Two ringy-dingys. A gracious good morning to you. Have I reached the party to whom I am speaking?"   **A: Lily Tomlin**

10. What famed gangster claimed, "When I sell my liquor, it's called bootlegging; when my patrons serve it on Lake Shore Drive, it's called hospitality"?   **A: Al Capone**

11. What famous children's author wrote in "The Lorax," "Unless someone like you cares a whole awful lot, nothing is going to get better. It's not"?   **A: Dr. Seuss (Theodor Geisel**

12. What much-admired former First Lady wrote, "No one can make you feel inferior without your consent"?   **A: Eleanor Roosevelt**

13. What 19th century humorist and author quipped, "Always do right. This will gratify some people and astonish the rest"?

A: Mark Twain

14. What founding father stated, "I believe that banking institutions are more dangerous to our liberties than standing armies"?   **A: Thomas Jefferson**

15. This U.S. diplomat, inventor, politician and printer quipped, "He that falls in love with himself will have no rivals."   **A: Benjamin Franklin**

16. What 19th century Irish dramatist said, "Always forgive your enemies; nothing annoys them so much"?   **A: Oscar Wilde**

17. What ancient Greek philosopher said, "A flatterer is a friend who is your inferior, or pretends to be so"?   **A: Aristotle**

18. What famed civil rights leader said, "In the end, we will remember not the words of our enemies, but the silence of our

friends"?   **A: Martin Luther King Jr.**

19. This Chinese philosopher said, "Before you embark on a journey of revenge, dig two graves."   **A: Confucius**

20. What Irish satirist wrote, ". . .A young healthy child well nursed is at a year old a most delicious, nourishing and wholesome food, whether stewed, roasted, baked or boiled, and I make no doubt that it will equally serve in a fricassee, or a ragout"?

A: Jonathan Swift (A Modest Proposal)

21. What American transcendentalist noted, "Any fool can make a rule, and any fool will mind it"?   **A: Henry David Thoreau**

22. This French leader said, "Glory is fleeting, but obscurity is forever."   **A: Napoleon Bonaparte**

23. What famous singer said, "I don't know anything about music. In my line you don't have to"?   **A: Elvis Presley**

24. What author of "Old Possum's Book of Practical Cats" quipped, "Some editors are failed writers, but so are most writers"?

A: T. S. Eliot

25. What WWII general famously said, "We are not retreating – we are advancing in another direction"?   **A: General Douglas MacArthur**

RELIGION

1. What pioneer media evangelist preached the gospel from her Foursquare Angelus Temple in the 1930s?   **A: Aimee Semple McPherson**

2. This organization has distributed free Bibles in hotel rooms, hospitals and schools since 1908.   **A: Gideons International**

3. Because of her lawsuit which ended Bible reading in public schools, Life magazine referred to her as "the most hated woman in America" in 1964.   **A: Madalyn Murray O'Hair**

4. This English Lord High Chancellor was convicted of treason and beheaded after he refused to acknowledge King Henry VIII as Supreme Head of the Church of England.   **A: Sir Thomas More**

5. What ancient sacred texts, whose name means "knowledge," are the oldest scriptures of Hinduism?   **A: Vedas**

6. Body marks or sensations of pain that correspond to the wounds of Jesus on the cross are referred to by what term?   **A: Stigmata**

7. Which denomination of Islam constitutes about 90% of the world's Muslim population?   **A: Sunni**

8. What is the term for the political movement that supports the establishment of a Jewish homeland in the Holy Land? **A: Zionism**

9. The holiest day of the Jewish year is this Jewish Day of Atonement.   **A: Yom Kippur**

10. What Christian denomination is best known for its door-to-door preaching, distribution of The Watchtower and refusal of blood transfusions?   **A: Jehovah's Witnesses**

11. What 18th century Anglican minister is credited with founding the Methodist denomination?   **A: John Wesley**

12. What is the term for a messenger or an emissary of the Pope?

A: Legate

13. What Christian saint, martyred by Roman Emperors Diocletian and Maximilian in 303, was the patron saint of dancers?   **A: St. Vitus**

14. Male adherents of this religion have "Singh" as their last name while females have "Kaur."   **A: Sikhism**

15. What Semitic dialect was spoken by Jesus Christ during his ministry in the first century?   **A: Aramaic**

16. What giant Philistine warrior of the Bible probably stood 6'9"?   **A: Goliath**

17. Known as the Piscatory Ring or The Fisherman's Ring, this ring featuring a bas-relief of Peter fishing from a boat is an official part of whose regalia?   **A: The Pope**

18. What system of subterranean burial vaults served as tombs for early Christians?   **A: Catacombs**

19. What Christian denomination traces its roots back to the teachings of French theologian John Calvin through Scotsman John Knox in England and Scotland?   **A: Presbyterianism**

20. What world-renowned American evangelist founded a famous Bible Institute in the Near North Side of Chicago in 1886?   **A: D. L. Moody**

21. This name of this anti-Israeli Shi'a Islamist group and political party formed in Lebanon in the 1980s literally means "Party of Allah."   **A: Hezbollah**

22. What sacred river that rises in the western Himalayas is the fifth most-polluted river in the world?   **A: Ganges**

23. What American founding father omitted all the miracles in his book "The Life and Morals of Jesus of Nazareth"?   **A: Thomas Jefferson**

24. What American evangelist has been on Gallup's list of most admired men and women 55 times since 1955, more than any other individual in the world?   **A: Billy Graham**

25. What biblical patriarch is considered to be the father of Judaism?   **A: Abraham**

ROCK, POP AND SOUL MUSIC

1. In 1999 she became the oldest female solo artist (age 52) to top the Billboard Hot 100 chart with her single "Believe." **A: Cher**

2. What American alt/indie rock band composed of three brothers and a cousin won a Grammy for "Best Rock Song" in 2010 for their hit "Use Somebody"? **A: Kings of Leon**

3. In 1969, this soul/R & B group became the first Motown recording act to win a Grammy – for "Cloud Nine." **A: The Temptations**

4. Whose early songs like "Blowin' in the Wind" and "The Times They Are a-Changin" became anthems for the American civil rights and anti-war movements? **A: Bob Dylan**

5. What Los Angeles band has topped Billboard's Hot Modern Rock Tracks with the most number one songs (12), the most cumulative weeks at number one (85), and the most top 10 songs (24)? **A: Red Hot Chili Peppers**

6. He was still a teenager when his hits "Itsy Bitsy Teenie Weenie Yellow Polka Dot Bikini" and "Sealed with a Kiss" topped the charts in the early 60s. **A: Brian Hyland**

7. What Spanish group is best known for its dance single "Macarena" which was released in early 1994? **A: Los del Rio**

8. What drummer made it to the top of Billboard charts with a record four bands: Nirvana, Foo Fighters, Queens of the Stone Age and Nine Inch Nails? **A: Dave Grohl**

9. What Englishwoman won a Grammy for "Best Rock & Roll Recording of 1964" for her hit "Downtown"?   **A: Petula Clark**

10. Whose first pop hit (1970) began, "It's a little bit funny, this feelin' inside"?   **A: Elton John ("Your Song")**

11. What critically-acclaimed 1966 Beach Boys album was one of the earliest rock "concept albums"?   **A: "Pet Sounds"**

12. Who topped the Alternative Songs chart in August 2013 with her song "Royals," a condemnation of the luxurious lifestyle of contemporary artists?   **A: Lorde**

13. What song by Bill Haley & His Comets did not become popular until it was chosen for the opening credits of the 1955 film "Blackboard Jungle"?   **A: "Rock Around the Clock"**

14. What California band is credited with reviving mainstream interest in punk rock in the U.S. with their 1994 debut album "Dookie"?   **A: Green Day**

15. Their pop-folk hit "Tom Dooley" from their first album in 1958 sold over three million copies.   **A: The Kingston Trio**

16. When this English punk rock bank was inducted into the Rock and Roll Hall of Fame in 2006, they refused to attend, calling the museum "a piss stain."   **A: Sex Pistols**

17. Whose song "(Sittin' On) The Dock of the Bay" became the first posthumous number one record on the Billboard Hot 100 chart?   **A: Otis Redding**

18. His hit "Livin' la Vida Loca" began the Latin pop explosion of 1999 and made him world famous.   **A: Ricky Martin**

19. This "Queen of Soul" became the first female performer to be inducted into the rock and Roll Hall of Fame.   **A: Aretha Franklin**

20. Sting wrote this song – the biggest hit of 1983 – essentially about stalking a lost lover.   **A: "Every Breath You Take"**

21. What "blue-eyed soul" icon of the Swinging Sixties had hits with "Son of a Preacher Man" and "Wishin' and Hopin'"?   **A: Dusty Springfield**

22. This former member of NSYNC established his solo career with the 2002 hits "Cry Me a River" and "Rock Your Body."   **A: Justin Timberlake**

23. Whose debut album, "Baby One More Time," is listed by "Guinness World Records" as being the best-selling debut album by a teenage solo artist?   **A: Britney Spears**

24. Also their lead vocalist, he composed many songs for "Queen," including "Bohemian Rhapsody," and "Crazy Little Thing Called Love."   **A: Freddie Mercury**

25. What Italian-American composer is best remembered for his film and television scores, including "Days of Wine and Roses" and "Breakfast at Tiffany's" with the hit song "Moon River"?   **A: Henry Mancini**

SCIENCE

1. Ethylene glycol is the primary ingredient in this automotive substance.   **A: Antifreeze**

2. Named after the Roman god of fire, this process makes rubber more durable.   **A: Vulcanization**

3. What is the most common element in the crust of the earth?
A: Oxygen

4. What is the term for a substance consisting of atoms with the same number of protons that cannot be chemically decomposed into simpler substances?   **A: Element**

5. What is the term for the transfer of fluid from an area of higher concentration to an area of lower concentration, usually through a membrane?   **A: Osmosis**

6. Any material able to decompose or be broken down by the earth's natural processes is given this term.   **A: Biodegradable**

7. What large lake fed by glacial meltwater covered much of Manitoba, northwestern Ontario, northern Minnesota, eastern North Dakota and Saskatchewan 13,000 years ago?   **A: Lake Agassiz**

8. What negatively charged particle moves in an orbit around the nucleus of an atom?   **A: Electron**

9. What is the term for a substance that accelerates a chemical reaction without becoming a part of the end product of the reaction?   **A: Catalyst**

10. A typical species becomes extinct within how many million years of its first appearance? **A: Ten million**

11. What unit of power is named after the Scottish scientist who developed the steam engine? **A: Watt (James Watt)**

12. What is the term for a reflected sound wave? **A: Echo**

13. What instrument was used primarily to determine the angle between an astronomical object and the horizon for navigation purposes? **A: Sextant**

14. What element has the chemical symbol "Cu"? **A: Copper**

15. What element is the lightest element on the periodic table and has the smallest atomic weight? **A: Hydrogen**

16. Which layer of the earth's atmosphere absorbs 97 – 99% of the sun's ultraviolet radiation, preventing it from damaging life forms on earth's surface? **A: Ozone**

17. What English naturalist explained how the fittest of each species survived through natural selection? **A: Charles Darwin**

18. What American botanist taught southern farmers to rotate cotton crops with legumes like peanuts and peas to restore soil fertility? **A: George Washington Carver**

19. The atomic number of an element is determined by the number of these in its nucleus. **A: Protons**

20. What element is used as an x-ray contrast agent for imaging the human gastrointestinal tract? **A: Barium**

21. What is the term for organisms – many of them microscopic – that cannot swim against a current and that are the main food source for many large fish and whales?   **A: Plankton**

22. This term means the measurement of the force of gravity on a human body.   **A: Weight**

23. An electric current that reverses direction periodically is called this.   **A: Alternating current**

24. What term is used for the scientific measure of the average kinetic energy of a group of particles?   **A: Temperature**

25. What is the term for the process of heating milk and other liquid foods to kill bacteria that may be harmful to humans?

A: Pasteurization

26. French for "little wing," these flight control mechanisms on the wings of aircraft are used to bank or roll the plane.   **A: Ailerons**

27. What is the term for the scientific study of the properties, distribution, and circulation of water?   **A: Hydrology**

28. What branch of science deals with describing, classifying and identifying organisms?   **A: Taxonomy**

29. What is the term for an icicle-like mineral formation that hangs from the ceiling of a cave?   **A: Stalactite**

30. What is the electrical term for any material that resists the flow of current?   **A: Insulator**

31. What instrument, generally interchangeable with "speed-ometer," measures the rotation speed of a shaft or disk?

A: Tachometer

32. What widely-used instrument measures ionizing radiation?

A: Geiger counter

33. An atom which has gained electrons, giving it a net negative charge, is known as this.   **A: Anion**

34. The book "Principles of Natural Philosophy" (Principia) lays out what physicist's laws of motion and universal gravitation?   **A: Sir Isaac Newton**

35. The "Fat Man" bomb used to bomb Nagasaki in 1945 had a core made of this radioactive element.   **A: Plutonium**

36. Rock carvings, especially those made by prehistoric people, are referred to by what term?   **A: Petroglyphs**

37. What is the biological term for the process of cell division by which identical daughter cells are produced?   **A: Mitosis**

38. A detergent is an example of this compound that lowers the surface tension between two liquids and increases its wetting properties.   **A: Surfactant**

39. Alcohol which has additives to make it poisonous, bad-tasting and foul-smelling to discourage human consumption is referred to by this term.   **A: Denatured alcohol**

40. What element is considered to be the chemical basis of all known life?   **A: Carbon**

41. What famous trial was precipitated by a substitute teacher teaching from a chapter in "Civic Biology" in Dayton, Tennessee in the spring of 1925?   **A: Scopes Monkey Trial or The State of Tennessee v. John Thomas Scopes**

42. What is the term for the application of science to industry or commerce?   **A: Technology**

43. What scale is used to measure acidity or alkalinity on a scale from 0 to 14?   **A: pH**

44. The U. S. Constitution is stored under what humidified inert gas to avoid degradation?   **A: Argon**

45. What is the term for the manipulation of DNA using biotech- nology to produce new types of organisms?   **A: Genetic engineering**

46. What hydrocarbon is responsible for the orange color of the carrot and the yellow coloration of milk-fat and butter?

A: Carotene

47. What is the scientific term for the ratio of the density of a substance to that of a standard substance (usually water)?

A: Specific gravity

48. What is the term for the close relationship between two organisms of different species, where both partners benefit from the association?   **A: Symbiosis**

49. A biologist specializing in the study of fungi and their properties is called what?   **A: Mycologist**

50. What chemical element is named for the Greek god of the Sun?   **A: Helium (Helios)**

SPORTS

1. Also called "caving," this term for the recreational pastime of exploring cave systems is derived from the Latin word for cave.

A: Spelunking (L. spelunca)

2. This 3,200 meter race is Australia's most celebrated horse race and one of the richest turf races with a purse of over $6 million.

A: Melbourne Cup

3. What Norwegian-American football coach made Notre Dame a major factor in college football during his 13 years as head coach, but died in 1931 when his plane crashed on his way to participate in the production of "The Spirit of Notre Dame"?   **A: Knute Rockne**

4. What woman, founder of the Women's Tennis Association, became the first woman to be named "Sports Illustrated Sportsperson of the Year" (1972)?   **A: Billie Jean King**

5. On September 14, 1990, this father and son pair of Seattle Mariners hit back to back home runs, the only time in major league history this has happened.   **A: Ken Griffeys Sr. and Jr.**

6. Before his death in 2001 in a crash at Daytona International Speedway, this NASCAR driver known as "The Intimidator" had won 76 Winston Cup races and seven NASCAR Winston Cup championships.   **A: Dale Earnhardt Sr.**

7. What word is used to describe the races on the same day that precede a major or important race?   **A: Undercard**

8. What Hall of Fame pitcher was the only major league player to have his number retired by three different teams? (Angels, Rangers, Astros)   **A: Nolan Ryan**

9. How long is the second limit on the shot clock in the NBA and the WNBA?   **A: 24 seconds**

10. With a win in Super Bowl VII in 1972, this AFC team became the only NFL team to complete a perfect season.   **A: Miami Dolphins**

11. What Eastern Conference team has won the most Stanley cup championships (11) of any U.S.-based NHL franchise?   **A: Detroit Red Wings**

12. What Hall of Fame pro baseball catcher was famous for his malapropisms such as "Texas has a lot of electrical votes"?

A: Yogi Berra

13. What professional heavyweight boxer was crowned "Sportsman of the Century" by "Sports Illustrated"? **A: Muhammad Ali**

14. What ground-breaking second baseman was the first recipient of the "Rookie of the Year Award" in MLB in 1947?   **A: Jackie Robinson**

15. Who is the NBA's all-time leading scorer with 38,387 points over a 20-year career?   **A: Kareem Abdul-Jabbar**

16. What AFC East team is the only NFL team to lose four consecutive Super Bowls?   **A: Buffalo Bills**

17. What NCAA Division 1 school's teams compete as the Crimson Tide?   **A: University of Alabama**

18. The NASCAR racing series formerly known as the Grand National Series (1950-1970) and the Winston Cup Series (1971 – 2003) are now known as what?   **A: Sprint Cup Series**

19. What is the term for a period of play in polo?   **A: Chukka**

20. What Swedish figure skater won the World Figure Skating Championships ten times from 1901 to 1911 and has a full-rotation jump named in his honor?   **A: Ulrich Salchow**

21. What is the term for the material(s) such as feathers attached to arrows to stabilize them aerodynamically?   **A: Fletching**

22. "The Big Three" pro golfers who popularized and commercialized the sport of golf during the 1960s are Jack Nicklaus, Gary Player and this man.   **A: Arnold Palmer**

23. What thoroughbred in 2015 became the first Triple Crown winner since Affirmed in 1978?   **A: American Pharoah**

24. What Norwegian figure skater and later film star introduced innovative skating techniques using dance choreography that revolutionized the sport of figure skating in the 1920s and 30s?   **A: Sonja Henie**

25. What Midwestern city is the smallest market with a major league sports team in North America?   **A: Green Bay, Wisconsin**

26. With what NFL team did elusive running back Barry Sanders spend his entire professional career?   **A: Detroit Lions**

27. What outdoor sport did author Izaak Walton call "The Contemplative Man's Recreation"?   **A: Fly fishing**

28. The third and final boxing match between heavyweight boxers Joe Frazier and Muhammad Ali in Araneta Coliseum in the Philippines in 1975 was given what nickname? **A: Thrilla in Manila**

29. What NCAA Division 1 athletic team's name was derived from the Greek/Latin phrase "Hoya Saxa" ("What Rocks")?

A: Georgetown University

30. What pro basketball power forward, nicknamed "The Mailman," had his number retired by the Utah Jazz in 2006?

A: Karl Malone

31. What basketball legend was known as the "Clown Prince" of the Harlem Globetrotters for 22 years and 16,000 games?

A: Meadowlark Lemon

32. The circular huddle used by basketball, football and cricket players originated at this university in 1892 when quarterback Paul D. Hubbard realized the opposing teams were reading his hand signals.   **A: Gallaudet**

33. What is the term for a dive in which the diver performs a backward somersault, entering the water feet first?   **A: Gainer**

34. What Canadian is the leading scorer in NHL history?

A: Wayne Gretzky

35. In 1907, Australian Annette Kellerman popularized this sport when she performed as an underwater ballerina in a glass tank in the New York Hippodrome.   **A: Synchronized swimming**

36. In tennis, a ball that is returned before it bounces is called what?   **A: Volley**

37. What 15-year-old Swiss girl became the youngest ever professional tennis Grand Slam champion in 1996?   **A: Martina Hingis**

38. What sailing yacht race awards the oldest international sporting trophy?   **A: America's Cup**

39. The Scottish 9th Marquess of Queensberry is well-known because the rules of what sport were named after him? **A: Boxing**

40. The British call the extremely rare score of three strokes under par on a hole an albatross, but Americans call it this.   **A: Double eagle**

41. What is the football term for tackling the opposing team's ball carrier in his own end zone?   **A: Safety**

42. The oldest American college football bowl game, usually played on New Year's Day, is played at a stadium in this California city.

A: Pasadena (Rose Bowl)

43. The major league baseball award for the best pitcher in each league is called what?   **A: Cy Young Award**

44. The motto of the Olympics is the Latin expression "Citius, altius, fortius," which means what?   **A: Faster, higher, stronger**

45. What 1948 Triple Crown winner was the first horse in history to win one million dollars?   **A: Citation**

46. What champion tennis playing sisters became the first African-American women to hold ownership in an NFL franchise when they became minority owners of the Miami Dolphins in 2009?

A: Venus and Serena Williams

47. What pro basketball player is the only player to score 100 points in a single NBA game?   **A: Wilt Chamberlain**

48. What is the nickname of the competitive sport of rowing an 8-person shell with a coxswain?   **A: Crew**

49. In what Greek city were the ancient Olympic Games held?

A: Olympia

50. What style of Olympic wrestling forbids holds below the waist?   **A: Greco-Roman**

TELEVISION

1. Her talk show, nationally syndicated from 1986 to 2011, made her the richest African-American of the 20th century and earned her the Presidential Medal of Freedom.   **A: Oprah Winfrey**

2. What former New York City mayor followed Judge Joseph Wapner as arbiter on the arbitration-based reality show "The People's Court" in 1997?   **A: Ed Koch**

3. What long-time variety show's 1948 debut featured Dean Martin and Jerry Lewis and Broadway composers Richard Rodgers and Oscar Hammerstein II previewing "South Pacific"?   **A: "The Ed Sullivan Show" ("Toast of the Town")**

4. Prior to hosting a popular ABC late-night talk show, he co-hosted "Win Ben Stein's Money" and "The Man Show."   **A: Jimmy Kimmel**

5. What breed of dog received a boost in popularity from Martin Crane's dog Eddie on the NBC sitcom "Frasier"?   **A: Jack Russell Terrier**

6. What long-time music performance show featured the segment "Rate-a-Record," which gave rise to the phrase "It's got a good beat and you can dance to it"?   **A: "American Bandstand"**

7. Which South Park character died in nearly every episode for the first five years of the show's run?   **A: Kenny**

8. Captains James T. Kirk and Jean-Luc Picard commanded this starship on "Star Trek."   **A: Enterprise**

9. What 1972 – 1985 BBC sitcom featured the staff of the ladies'
and gentlemen's clothing floor departments of the London
department store Grace Brothers?　**A: "Are You Being Served?"**

10. What former actress in 1962 became the first woman to run a
major television studio, which produced successful TV series like
"Star Trek" and "Mission: Impossible"?　**A: Lucille Ball**

11. He played the "Saturday Night Live" character Jack Handey with
his "Deep Thoughts" and "Fuzzy Memories," then went on to
become the United States Senator from Minnesota.　**A: Al
Franken**

12. Since it first broke into the Nielsen Top 20 ratings during the
1976-77 season, this CBS newsmagazine program is the most
successful program in U.S. television history.　**A: "60 Minutes"**

13. Who wrote or adapted nearly two-thirds of "The Twilight
Zone's" 156 episodes, and narrated all of them?　**A: Rod Serling**

14. What long-running NBC sitcom featured the theme song,
"Where Everybody Knows Your Name"?　**A: Cheers**

15. Who was the original host of the game show "Jeopardy," which
ran from March, 1964 to January, 1975?　**A: Art Fleming**

16. He was the talented handyman on "Captain Kangaroo," named
after his distinctively-colored overalls – although the show was
black and white for most of its run.　**A: Mr. Green Jeans**

17. What American soap opera featuring the Horton family aired its
12,000th episode in January of 2013?　**A: "Days of Our Lives"**

18. Who since 1982 has been the fashionable hostess of the longest-running syndicated game show in the U.S.?   **A: Vanna White (Wheel of Fortune)**

19. What actress is best known for her 19-year run as the saloon proprietress "Miss Kitty" on the television western "Gunsmoke"? **A: Amanda Blake**

20. What NBC singing competition hosted by Carson Daly began with "blind" auditions, then progressed to "battle rounds" and "knockout rounds"?   **A: "The Voice"**

21. In November, 1954 Wisconsin Senator Joe McCarthy became the first guest on this long-running CBS Sunday morning political interview news program.   **A: "Face the Nation"**

22. Alison Arngrim played this spoiled, sharp-tongued daughter of the mercantile owners in Walnut Grove on the NBC show "Little House on the Prairie."   **A: Nellie Oleson**

23. What small farming town in Minnesota was the home town of Rose Nylund (Betty White) on the NBC sitcom "The Golden Girls"? **A: St. Olaf**

24. What famous person hosted "Death Valley Days," an anthology series featuring true stories of the American West, in 1964 and 1965?   **A: Ronald Reagan**

25. What was Dr. Derek Shepherd's (Patrick Dempsey) nickname on the long-running ABC medical drama "Grey's Anatomy"? **A: McDreamy**

26. Don Johnson popularized the "T-shirt under Italian sport coat with sockless loafers" look on this NBC crime drama series.

A: "Miami Vice"

27. What 2010 – 2016 CBS sitcom featured a couple who met in a Chicago Overeaters Anonymous group and fell in love? A: "Mike & Molly"

28. What ABC sitcom featured Marion Lorne in the supporting role of Aunt Clara, a forgetful, bumbling but lovable witch whose spells often ended disastrously? A: "Bewitched"

29. Herve Villechaize played what pint-sized but energetic sidekick on the ABC series "Fantasy Island"? A: Tattoo

30. What was the nickname of Samuel Powers (Dustin Diamond), the nerd of the group of schoolmates on NBC's "Saved by the Bell"? A: Screech

31. Who played Alice Kramden to Jackie Gleason's Ralph on the 50s sitcom "The Honeymooners"? A: Audrey Meadows

32. What 90s NBC sitcom popularized the phrases "Yada, yada, yada," "Festivus," and "No soup for you"? A: "Seinfeld"

33. "The Office" employees worked for what fictional paper company branch in Scranton, Pennsylvania? A: Dunder Mifflin

34. Who played Bob Hartley's man-chasing receptionist Carol on his 70s show "The Bob Newhart Show"? A: Marcia Wallace

35. What CBS sitcom about a working-class bigot ranked number one in the yearly Nielsen ratings from 1971 to 1976? A: "All in the Family"

36. What cast member of "The Big Bang Theory" actually has a PhD in neuroscience from UCLA?   A: **Mayim Bialik (Amy Farrah Fowler)**

37. Who played Peter Florrick, Juliana Marguiles disgraced husband on "The Good Wife"?   A: **Chris Noth**

38. What is the nickname of the oldest child of John and Olivia Walton, parents of "The Waltons"?   A: **John-Boy**

39. What is the famous catchphrase exclaimed by the announcer when contestants are selected from the studio audience on "The Price is Right"?   A: **"Come on down!"**

40. What ABC TV series from the '60s featured an ongoing search for a mysterious one-armed man?   A: **"The Fugitive"**

41. What long-running TV show always ends its opening sketch with "Live from New York . . ."?   A: **"Saturday Night Live"**

42. What was the Clampett family's term for their swimming pool on the CBS series "The Beverly Hillbillies"?   A: **Cement pond**

43. What country star narrated the "Dukes of Hazzard" and sang and played its theme song as well?   A: **Waylon Jennings**

44. What was the nickname of the towering butler on "The Addams Family," who answered the door with a deep bass "You rang?"
A: **Lurch**

45. What "Monty Python" co-founder played Basil Fawlty on the '70s BBC sitcom "Fawlty Towers"?   A: **John Cleese**

46. What family-oriented variety show of the late '70s featured the theme song, "It's time to play the music; It's time to light the

lights . . ."?   A: **"The Muppet Show"**

47. What CBS science fiction series was responsible for the development of an entire constructed language – Klingon?

A: **"Star Trek"**

48. What actor played the beatnik Maynard G. Krebs on "The Many Loves of Dobie Gillis" and Gilligan on "Gilligan's Island"?   A: **Bob Denver**

49. What tool company sponsored Tim Taylor's (Tim Allen) "Tool Time" show on "Home Improvement?"   A: **Binford**

50. What NBC sitcom featured the theme song, "When the rain starts to pour / I'll be there for you / Like I've been there before / I'll be there for you/'cause you're there for me too . . . "?

A: **"Friends"**

TREES AND PLANTS

1. The generic name for rose oil, the essential oil extracted from rose petals for use in perfumery, is this.   **A: Attar of roses**

2. A group of Mormon settlers gave this southwestern yucca palm its nickname because its shape reminded them of a Biblical character reaching his hands up to the sky in prayer.   **A: Joshua tree**

3. What shrub, often referred to as a thorn apple, got its name from the old English term for hedge?   **A: Hawthorn**

4. What pungent shrub commonly found throughout the Southwest becomes tumbleweed when dried?   **A: Sagebrush**

5. The mission complex in San Antonio, Texas known as the Alamo was probably named for a grove of this type of trees nearby.

A: Cottonwood

6. The Canadian flag features a generic leaf of this tree representing ten species of this national emblem.   **A: Maple**

7. In vascular plants, xylem tissue transports water. What transport tissue carries sucrose?   **A: Phloem**

8. What is the botanical term for the fruit of the peach, cherry, apricot and plum?   **A: Drupe**

9. Cultivation of this bulbous plant in the lily family probably began in Persia as early as the 10th century, before its first mention by the Persian poet Omar Khayyám in the 11th century.   **A: Tulip**

10. What oil-burning device is used to prevent frost in orchards by

forming a blanket of smog?   **A: Smudge pot**

11. What is the term for the tendency of young sunflower buds to track the sun during the day?   **A: Heliotropism**

12. What medicinal plant's name means "pretty woman" in Italian because of its use in eye-drops to seductively dilate the pupils of the eyes?   **A: Belladonna**

13. The cautionary mnemonic "Leaflets three; let it be" usually applies to the plant toxicodendron radicans, more commonly known as what?   **A: Poison ivy**

14. What showy-flowered shrub's name comes from the ancient Greek meaning "rose tree"?   **A: Rhododendron**

15. Luther Burbank developed this flowering perennial and named it after a California mountain because its petals were the color of the snow.   **A: Shasta daisy**

16. Ornithophily is the pollination of flowering plants by what?
A: Birds

17. What Swedish botanist founded the modern system of classifying organisms and is known as the "Father of modern taxonomy"?   **A: Carl Linnaeus**

18. What is the term for a saguaro cactus without arms?   **A: Spear**

19 This deciduous tree with heart-shaped leaves is called a lime or linden tree in Britain.   **A: Basswood**

20. The state flower of Minnesota is the "showy" variety of this wild orchid.   **A: Lady's slipper**

21. Southern farmers were paid $8 per acre to plant this perennial vine to stop soil erosion in the 1930s and '40s, but now it's an invasive noxious weed throughout the South.   **A: Kudzu vine**

22. What is the term for the reddish fruit of the wild rose plant?

A: Rose hips

23. What common species of wild iris (Iris versicolor) can be found in marshes and along stream banks and shores in the Eastern U.S. and Canada?   **A: Blue flag**

24. Lt. James Cook wrote of his decision to name this oceanic embayment on the Australian continent, "The great quantity of plants Mr. Banks and Dr. Solander found in this place occasioned my giving it the name of . . . ."   **A: Botany Bay**

25. Since the presence of seeds harms the quality of pineapple, Hawaii prohibits the importation of this pollinating bird.

A: Hummingbirds

U. S. HISTORY

1. Aviator Wiley Post and this humorist/motion picture actor both died in a small plane crash in northern Alaska in August of 1935. **A: Will Rogers**

2. This pro-independence political tract that George Washington had read to all his troops in 1776 remains the all-time best selling American title. **A: Common Sense**

3. Members of the American Indian Movement occupied this historic community in South Dakota in 1973 to protest abuse and corruption by the Pine Ridge tribal president and the American government's failure to fulfill treaties. **A: Wounded Knee**

4. What civil rights activists violated state and local Jim Crow laws by desegregating buses in the early 1960s? **A: Freedom Riders**

5. Julius and Ethel Rosenberg were executed in Sing Sing in 1953 for conspiracy to commit this crime. **A: Espionage**

6. The Saint Valentine's Day Massacre in Chicago in 1929 was a result of the struggle between the organized crime gangs of Bugs Moran and who? **A: Al Capone**

7. Members of the Ohio National Guard fired 67 rounds into a crowd of unarmed students in May of 1970, killing four students of this university and wounding nine. **A: Kent State**

8. When Christopher Columbus arrive in Puerto Rico in November of 1493, he named the island San Juan Bautista in honor of what Catholic saint? **A: John the Baptist**

9. A siege of the compound of this religious group in 1993 resulted in the death of David Koresh and 82 of his followers. **A: Branch Davidians**

10. What was the name for the aftermath of the Napoleonic Wars when the Democratic-Republican party led by President James Monroe was unchallenged by a major political rival? **A: The Era of Good Feeling**

11. What section of Los Angeles was devastated by rioting and looting in August, 1965 due to outrage and unrest over police racism and unemployment? **A: Watts**

12. What was the term for the shanty towns occupied by homeless families during the Great Depression? **A: Hoovervilles**

13. What American oil company was dissolved in 1911 when the U. S. Supreme Court ruled that it was an illegal monopoly?

A: Standard Oil

14. What influential Chicago mayor was blamed for the brutal police repression used to break up protests outside the 1968 Democratic National Convention? **A: Richard J. Daley**

15. What revolutionary group of African Americans advocated the use of violence and guerilla tactics for remedying racial injustices between 1966 and 1982? **A: Black panthers**

16. What Niagara Falls neighborhood was evacuated in 1978 due to the discovery of Hooker Chemical's burial of 22,000 tons of toxic waste beneath its structures? **A: Love Canal**

17. What Boston nightclub was the scene of the deadliest nightclub fire in history when 492 patrons were killed in November of 1942?   **A: Cocoanut Grove**

18. What is the term for the ethnic group of people in Southern Louisiana consisting of the exiled descendants of French speakers from Acadia (The Maritime Provinces of Eastern Canada)? **A: Cajun**

19. What Ohio town is the namesake of an acute viral gastroenteritis that plagues cruise ship passengers almost every year?   **A: Norwalk**

20. An "argonaut" is a person who took part in what historic 1849 event?   **A: California gold rush**

21. What federal law passed in 1862 gave 160 acres of land to anyone who settled on and farmed the land for five years?

A: Homestead Act

22. What publishing heiress was kidnapped by the terrorist group Symbionese Liberation Army in early 1974?   **A: Patty Hearst**

23. What was the slang term for saloons that illegally sold alcoholic beverages during Prohibition?   **A: Speakeasies**

24. What governing document was signed by 41 male passengers aboard ship in Provincetown Harbor, Cape Cod, in 1620?

A: Mayflower Compact

25. What Founding Father became wealthy publishing "Poor Richard's Almanack" and "The Pennsylvania Gazette"?

A: Benjamin Franklin

26. What saloon-keeper and Justice of the Peace in Val Verde County, Texas called himself "The Law West of the Pecos"?

A: Judge Roy Bean

27. What was the term used to describe President Franklin Roosevelt's 30 evening radio addresses during the Great Depression?   **A: Fireside Chats**

28. In 1904, the passenger steamboat General Slocum caught fire and sank in this New York City river, killing 1,021 of its passengers on a church picnic.   **A: East River**

29. What was the name of the first U. S. nuclear-powered submarine, launched in 1954 and currently preserved as a museum in Groton, Connecticut?   **A: USS Nautilus**

30. He was the publisher of the New York Weekly Journal whose acquittal for criticizing the colonial governor William Cosby helped establish freedom of the press in America.   **A: John Peter Zenger**

31. What terrorist faction of Students for a Democratic Society conducted a campaign of bombings through the mid-70s targeting government buildings?   **A: Weather Underground or Weathermen**

32. What New York politician, "boss" of Tammany Hall and the 19th century political patronage machine, died in the Ludlow Street Jail in 1878?   **A: William M. Tweed**

33. What federal building in Oklahoma City was the target of a domestic terrorist bomb attack on April 19, 1995, killing 168 people and causing $652 million worth of damage?   **A: Alfred P. Murrah**

34. What U. S. agency was created by President Harry S Truman in July of 1947, spurred by the unforeseen attack on Pearl Harbor and the need for the coordination of intelligence efforts?   **A: Central Intelligence Agency**

35. What term, coined by Mark Twain, characterized the late19th century as an era of abject poverty masked by highly concentrated wealth?   **A: The Gilded Age**

36. What term was a common name for the burial grounds of gunfighters in the American West?   **A: Boot Hill**

37. What 19th century doctrine held that Americans were exceptional and destined to expand across North America to bring agrarian civilization to the West?   **A: Manifest Destiny**

38. What annual prize established in 1917 for achievements in journalism, literature and musical composition is administered by Columbia University?   **A: Pulitzer Prize**

39. What U. S. space shuttle broke apart 73 seconds into its tenth mission on January 28, 1986, killing all seven crew members?

A: Challenger

40. Members of this madman's "family" killed nine people in the summer of 1969, including pregnant actress Sharon Tate?

A: Charles Manson

41. What acronym originated in the 1980s to describe young, college-educated, urban adults who were out of touch with lower-income Middle America? **A: Yuppie (young urban professional)**

42. What American aviation pioneer and early supporter of the Equal Rights Amendment was the first female aviator to fly solo across the Atlantic Ocean? **A: Amelia Earhart**

43. More than ten thousand Native Americans died due to this forced relocation from their ancestral homelands following the Indian Removal Act of 1830. **A: Trail of Tears**

44. U. S. Chief Justice Roger B. Taney ruled that any person descended from Africans is not a citizen of the U.S. in this controversial 1857 case. **A: Dred Scott**

45. What New York City skyscraper designed and built in Art Deco style in 1931 was designated as a National Historic Landmark in 1986? **A: Empire State Building**

46. A 1998 DNA study strongly supported the conclusion that Thomas Jefferson was the father of her six illegitimate children. **A: Sally Hemings**

47. What New York Whig became president upon the death of Zachary Taylor in July, 1850? **A: Millard Fillmore**

48. What cemetery was established during the Civil War on the estate – purchased at a tax sale for $26,800 – of Confederate General Robert E. Lee? **A: Arlington National Cemetery**

49. In1902 this First Lady became the first American woman to be honored on a U.S. postage stamp.   **A: Martha Washington**

50. The engraving and design departments of the U.S. Mint are located at the facility in this city.   **A: Philadelphia**

WAR AND THE MILITARY

1. What is the Japanese word for "divine wind," the term for planes carrying out suicide attacks against Allied ships in WWII?

A: Kamikaze

2. What country engaged the United Kingdom in a ten-week war over the Falkland Islands, South Georgia and the South Sandwich Islands in 1982?   **A: Argentina**

3. What nickname was given by the mainstream media to President Reagan's proposed Strategic Defense Initiative missile defense system?   **A: Star Wars**

4. What war was the subject of Alfred, Lord Tennyson's poem "The Charge of the Light Brigade"?   **A: Crimean War**

5. What is the term for a petty officer who performs chiefly clerical duties in the U.S. Navy?   **A: Yeoman**

6. What was the acronym for the WWII women's branch of the U. S. Coast Guard Reserve?   **A: SPARS**

7. What Mexican president launched an assault on the Alamo Mission in 1836, killing all its defenders?   **A: President General Antonio Lopez de Santa Anna**

8. What is the name given to a series of wars between the Houses of Lancaster and York between 1455 and 1487?   **A: Wars of the Roses**

9. This rapid-fire gun was first used in warfare during the Civil War (1864) when Union commanders purchased twelve of them with personal funds.   **A: Gatling gun**

10. What Russian warriors of czarist times were noted for their horsemanship and military skill?   **A: Cossacks**

11. In World War I, what was the term for a psychiatric illness caused by injury to the nerves during combat?   **A: Shell shock**

12. July 14th commemorates the storming of a prison in 1789 in France. What is the day called?   **A: Bastille Day**

13. What four-star admiral and member of the Joint Chiefs of Staff reports directly to the civilian Secretary of the Navy?   **A: Chief of Naval Operations**

14. What is the term for a student at a military school who is training to be an officer?   **A: Cadet**

15. World War I was known by this nickname, especially before World War II came along.   **A: Great War**

16. What French aristocrat and military officer is buried in a Paris cemetery under soil from Bunker Hill?   **A: Gilbert du Motier (Marquis de Lafayette)**

17. The French and Spanish fleets lost 22 ships, while Admiral Lord Nelson lost none in this decisive naval battle of 1805.   **A: Battle of Trafalgar**

18. What is the military term for assembling troops for inspection?   **A: Muster**

19. Fewer than 1,000 Israelis were killed compared to 20,000 Arab forces in this June, 1967 war.   **A: Six-Day War**

20. The wreck of this battleship remains at Pearl Harbor to commemorate the 1,177 crew members lost in the December 7, 1941 Japanese attack on Pearl Harbor.   **A: USS Arizona**

21. What British ocean liner was torpedoed and sunk off the coast of Ireland by a German U-boat in May of 1915, killing 1,198 passengers and crew?   **A: RMS Lusitania**

22. What famed Revolutionary War site on the Schuylkill River was named for a small ironworks nearby?   **A: Valley Forge**

23. What late-1800s wars were fought by Britain and the descendants of Dutch settlers for the control of South Africa?

A: Boer Wars

24. What was the nickname for the first official national flag of the Confederacy?   **A: Stars and Bars**

25. What major 1968 Viet Cong offensive was named for the Vietnamese New Year when the first major attacks took place?

A: Tet Offensive

WORLD HISTORY

1. What Dutch exotic dancer and courtesan was executed for espionage by firing squad in France during World War I?

A: Mata Hari

2. What international organization founded in January, 1920, was the first to have the principal mission of maintaining world peace?   **A: League of Nations**

3. Russian General Secretary Mikhail Gorbachev encouraged what policy of "openness" during his 6-year administration?

A: Glasnost

4. In what Ukrainian city did the nuclear power plant reactor blow in April of 1986, releasing deadly radioactive material into the air?   **A: Chernobyl**

5. With what famous ocean luxury liner did the MS Stockholm collide off the coast of Nantucket in July, 1956, killing 46 passengers and crew?   **A: Andrea Doria**

6. From 1192 to 1867, Japan was ruled by these hereditary military dictators.   **A: Shoguns**

7. Queen Elizabeth I's mother was the Marquess of Pembroke. By what name is she better known?   **A: Anne Boleyn**

8. What system of societal structure prevalent in medieval Europe was characterized by the holding of land in exchange for labor or service?   **A: Feudalism**

9. What Russian term for a member of the Russian Social Democratic Labor Party faction literally meant "one of the majority"?

A: Bolshevik

10. Whose effigy is burned on a bonfire every 5th of November in Britain because of his involvement in the 1605 Gunpowder Plot?

A: Guy Fawkes

11. What city in India was the site of a deadly Union Carbide leak which killed 3,787 people in 1984?   A: Bhopal

12. The October, 1957 launch of what Soviet satellite triggered the Space Race between the United States and the Soviet Union?

A: Sputnik

13. A terrorist bomb in a suitcase caused Pan Am Flight 103 to explode over this Scottish city, killing all 243 passengers in December of 1988.   A: Lockerbie

14. What country's "Althing" or national parliament was founded in 930 and still holds sessions today?   A: Iceland

15. What ancient East Germanic tribe lent its name to describe senseless destruction such as the sacking and looting of Rome in 455?   A: Vandals

16. What is the term for the Cambodian sites where the Communist Khmer Rouge executed more than a million people in the late 1970s?   A: The Killing Fields

17. After 12 days of secret negotiations in 1978, Egyptian President Anwar Sadat and Israeli Prime Minister Menachem Begin signed a

peace treaty named after this country retreat.   **A: Camp David (Camp David Accords)**

18. What historical era followed the decline of the Roman Empire, when cultural, intellectual and economic deterioration blighted Western Europe?   **A: Dark Ages**

19. What international figure was the target of attempted assassin Mehmet Ali Agca in St. Peter's Square in 1981?   **A: Pope John Paul II**

20. What term meaning "shuddering" was given to the Palestinian uprisings against Israeli occupation from the late 80s onward?
A: Intifada

21. What member of the Provisional Irish Republican Army died while on hunger strike at Maze Prison in May of 1981, sparking widespread protests?   **A: Bobby Sands**

22. The Piper Alpha oil rig disaster resulted in the death of 167 workers in this sea in 1988.   **A: North Sea**

23. What French revolutionary is credited with masterminding the "Reign of Terror" as leader of France's Committee of Public Safety?   **A: Maximilian Robespierre**

24. What Scottish missionary and explorer of Africa failed to find the source of the Nile but discovered Victoria Falls and numerous other geographical features for Western science?   **A: Dr. David Livingstone**

25. What was the name of the state formed to block German expansion by the uniting of Denmark, Norway and Sweden from 1397 to 1523?   **A: Kalmar Union**

.

63604770R00089

Made in the USA
Lexington, KY
11 May 2017